WITHDRAWN
HARVARD LIBRARY
WITHDRAWN

Professional Morality and Guilty Bystanding

Professional Morality and Guilty Bystanding: Merton's *Conjectures* and the Value of Work

By

Barry L. Padgett

BJ
1498
.P33
2009

Professional Morality and Guilty Bystanding: Merton's *Conjectures* and the Value of Work,
By Barry L. Padgett

This book first published 2009

Cambridge Scholars Publishing

12 Back Chapman Street, Newcastle upon Tyne, NE6 2XX, UK

British Library Cataloguing in Publication Data
A catalogue record for this book is available from the British Library

Copyright © 2009 by Barry L. Padgett

All rights for this book reserved. No part of this book may be reproduced, stored in a retrieval system, or transmitted, in any form or by any means, electronic, mechanical, photocopying, recording or otherwise, without the prior permission of the copyright owner.

ISBN (10): 1-4438-0245-X, ISBN (13): 978-1-4438-0245-1

Table of Contents

Preface vii

Acknowledgements xi

Chapter One 1
Professional Ethics and Thomas Merton

Chapter Two 13
Moral Theory and Professional Life

Chapter Three 37
Contemporary Challenges in Professional Ethics

Chapter Four 75
Professional Ethics and Moral Imagination

Chapter Five 99
Moral Imagination and Leadership

Notes 125

Bibliography 133

Index 137

Preface

In March, 2006 the Ethics and Social Justice Center of Bellarmine University, in collaboration with its Thomas Merton Center, hosted a conference on "Merton and Moral Reflection in the Professions," exploring the implications of Thomas Merton's *Conjectures of a Guilty Bystander* for professional morality. The conference drew a good number of participants from a variety of walks of life, including law, education, healthcare, and business, among other vocations.

The conference was inspired by the real-world story of Dr. Linda Peeno, whose experience as a medical reviewer for a major health insurance corporation is depicted in the movie *Damaged Care*. A pun on "managed care," the film portrays ethical dilemmas which Dr. Peeno and other healthcare professionals like her encounter on a daily basis. When she meets with a frustrated plaintiff's attorney and discovers that some of her decisions are not what they seem, their subsequent conversation turns to the contemplative moral insights of Thomas Merton. Finding spiritual direction and encouragement from his writings, Linda became a moral protester of the healthcare industry. She has testified before the Congress of the United States, has appeared on numerous television shows, given keynote addresses and conference presentations, and her story was recounted in Michael Moore's film, *Sicko*. Dr. Peeno discovered that many professionals like herself have found guidance and inspiration in Merton's writings. Our conference became a forum for many of their real-world stories.

The conference held at Bellarmine further confirmed the relevance of Merton's insights for contemporary times. Dr. Peeno's experience is not unique, but one of many that finds both comfort and confrontation in the writings of Thomas Merton. Like the old seminary saying that a minister should, "comfort the afflicted, and afflict the comforted," Merton's writings continue to offer solace during troubling times. But he also continues to challenge during times when one would otherwise be content and self-congratulatory from the comfort of accomplishments.

Such is the danger of professional life. Work has such an important role in our lives; it bears a standard by which we measure our success. It is a major component of self-actualization and well-being. However, our jobs can also be fraught with ethical conflicts and ambiguities; these become sources of frustration and alienation. What is needed is a transformation, a renewal of our professional lives and the institutional contexts in which we operate. To use a religious metaphor, we need a conversion experience that will humanize the alienating aspects of work and professions. I argue that Merton's call to contemplation is a means by which this conversion and subsequent transformation can take place. His reflections in *Conjectures of a Guilty Bystander* offer one the confidence to embark on a deeply spiritual journey that seeks to transcend the mountainous peaks which would divide the personal from the professional, and his insights give one hope that through reasoned moral action the negative features our organizations and workplaces can be transformed.

Contemplation, as Merton understands it, facilitates the maturation of character and lays the foundation for wisdom. Self-knowledge, which consists not only of critical self-reflection but also having a sense of one's purpose, constitutes the wisdom that Merton demonstrated on various issues, a wisdom rooted in contemplation. From *Conjectures of a Guilty Bystander* alone one can sense Merton's grasp of the big picture: regarding war, Christian social action, his views about communism and freedom, and his discussions of interfaith dialogue. Possessing self-understanding, coupled with an expansive and inclusive view of human reality, Merton exhibited tremendous leadership on these and other issues.

Leadership involves the use of moral imagination to create an environment in which open discussions about ethical conflicts can take place, especially without the fear (much less reality) of retribution or being ostracized. Moral imagination enables one to see that, without self-knowledge, a grasp of the big picture, or a unity of purpose, one is simply practicing a logic of failure, allowing an artificial separation of competitiveness and the potential for self-gain to override moral sensitivities. While excessive individualism and competitiveness may appear to lead to genuine success in the short term, in the long run these attitudes tend not to be conducive to well-being for individuals or the communities they inhabit.

Thomas Merton, though a cloistered monk, possessed an uncanny sense of self-awareness and moral imagination. His life and writings have inspired countless persons on their spiritual journeys. Yet, while people have looked to Merton for guidance on spiritual issues, the implications of his thought for several other areas of life are also open to exploration. Moreover, for persons who consider all other facets of life in light of their spiritual commitments, Merton's perspective is even more central to integrating the conflicting demands of modern life, particularly work, into a holistic perspective. Such was the case for Dr. Peeno, who recognized the ethical import of her daily job and, at that moment, realized that she stood at a crossroad: to carry on as usual, complying to the demands of those in high rank and power, or to exercise transformative leadership aimed at higher values and goals. Like Dr. Peeno, each day many professionals struggle to navigate the difficult ethical dilemmas that they confront in the workplace, moral conflicts that education did little to prepare them for, and for which they receive little support from the organizations that they serve.

This book is an exploration of these and other moral problems of professional life. The investigation begins with an examination of the meaning of work and a brief introduction to Thomas Merton, and then turns to the application of ethical theories to professions. From the perspective of several moral theories, the next step is to examine contemporary ethical challenges in professions, the sorts of dilemmas professionals encounter daily. The expedition then goes into more dense and less charted territory, the importance of moral imagination (in contrast to ethical theorizing) to one's moral compass. In complex terrain and in difficult circumstances, however, a compass is of little use without a map. So this exploration then turns to questions of leadership and, beyond edification of isolated individuals, the task of improving professions for everyone. Along the way, insights from Merton will serve as guideposts. I cannot overstress the metaphor of an expedition here. Although I may make an occasional controversial claim and explore various directions, I do not arrive at any fixed destination or major conclusion. As poet Frederick Smock states in his book, *Pax Intrantibus: A Meditation on the Poetry of Thomas Merton*, "Writing is an act of discovery for the writer—neither the outcome nor its meaning can be predetermined." This book is an initial step on a journey to discover the implications of Merton's insights for moral issues which arise in the context of our working lives. It is dedicated to all persons who share that journey.

ACKNOWLEDGEMENTS

I am deeply indebted to many people for the privilege of pursuing this topic. First and foremost, I am extremely grateful to Dr. Paul Pearson, director and archivist of the Merton Center at Bellarmine University, for his knowledge, wise council and sense of humor as I struggled with many of the ideas in Merton's writings as well as my own. I am also indebted to Lauren Titus, MFA, who read the manuscript several times, offering assistance with technical aspects, excellent critical comments, and many suggestions for improvement. Many others contributed to this work, in large and small ways. I am grateful to Drs. Mil Thompson, Evanthia Speliotis, Elizabeth Hinson-Hasty and especially to Frederick Smock for tolerating my occasional interruptions and impromptu discussions. These close colleagues have done their best to improve my perspective and articulation of ideas in this book; any misunderstandings or errors that remain are solely mine. Bellarmine University generously granted a sabbatical to me in order to complete this project.

I am grateful to Andy Nercessian and the helpful staff of Cambridge Scholars Press for their assistance in bringing this project to fruition. Some publishers of professional ethics literature have only passing interest in Merton studies; some publishers of Merton scholarship have little interest in the area of applied philosophy. Cambridge Scholars Press expressed an interest in both, allowing this promising direction of research to move forward.

The author also acknowledges the following publishers for permission to use these sources. The photograph of Thomas Merton used with permission of the Merton Legacy Trust and the Thomas Merton Center at Bellarmine University. Citations from Thomas Merton's *Conjectures of a Guilty Bystander* are reprinted with permission of Random House. Portions of Chapter Two were published by the author as, "The Importance of Cultural History" in *The Remnant Review* (Vol. 4, no. 1, 2008), journal of the Remnant Trust, Inc. Portions of Chapter Three were published by the author as a review article, "Making Good; How Young People Cope With Moral Dilemmas at Work," in the journal, *Business Ethics Quarterly* (Vol. 18, no. 2, April 2008), journal of the Society for Business Ethics.

I also wish to thank my father, who taught me the value of work; my mother, who instilled in me a capacity for contemplative reflection; and thanks to Kim, Martin and Grahame, who tolerated my "busy-ness" and contributed in no small way to my desire to improve the nature of work. There is a famous quotation from American Founder, John Adams: "I must study politics and war so that my sons may have the liberty to study mathematics and philosophy. My sons ought to study mathematics and philosophy . . . in order to give their children a right to study painting, poetry, music. . . ." In the spirit of Adams, I study philosophy and work in order that future generations may more closely approach the ideal of making work good.

Chapter One

Professional Ethics and Thomas Merton

A few years ago, administrators of the university where I work asked me to teach a senior-level leadership course with the title, "The Value of Work." Although the title struck me as problematic from a philosopher's point of view (not to mention from a student's point of view—who would want to take a class with that title?), I was very pleased to have been given this opportunity. It was a topic that I had been thinking about for a long time. Growing up on a small farm in rural Alabama informally introduced me to work at a very young age. I had the usual chores, everything from caring for our crops and farm animals to picking up rocks out of the pasture. (Acres of sloped hillside, it seemed to grow rocks almost as well as it did grass). Midway through high school I received the formal introduction to work, first at a feed mill and later as a busboy. After high school graduation I joined the workforce on a full-time basis. During those years of early adulthood, I occasionally changed jobs, some blue-collar and some white-collar, but it wasn't until my mid-twenties that I recognized the advantages of pursuing a college education. Although my father generously helped me to achieve my educational goals (which also changed occasionally), I always continued to work, at least part time, from my entrance into college all the way through graduate school. During my history of employment, I'd seen people happy and successful in their career achievements, and I'd seen people miserable and alienated by their daily jobs. An introspective awareness and an outward recognition of circumstances influenced my own sense of direction and led me to pursue a terminal degree that would allow me to maximize my chances of happiness and success in a career and—perhaps even more—to avoid the horrors of being miserably alienated for most of my adult life. So I was pleased at the invitation to teach a course on "The Value of Work," because it was a topic that had interested me for years, and not just in an intellectual sense. I had lived it, I was still living it; and I wasn't alone. Most adults struggle to resolve the value of work in their lives. Thus in planning for the course, I discussed it with many people, especially friends and family. My father-in-law, a paradigm of a blue-collar entrepreneur, gave me his thoughts on the subject of work. "I knew from the very first day," he quipped in Mark Twain fashion, "that I wasn't going to like it."

The sentiment of his expression was familiar to me. It captures not only the lack of fulfillment that many find in employment but also the demoralization that work can inflict upon an individual. Yet it also indicates the opposite, the ideal of meaningful work, of work providing an outward manifestation of who we are on the inside. There is a hope, a desire for work to be a source of personal well-being and self-actualization rather than a source of frustration, degradation or just "working for the weekend." This hope was particularly expressed in the wake of the Industrial Revolution of the late nineteenth and early twentieth centuries and continues to this day in themes of social justice. It finds expression from the philosophical writings of a young Karl Marx in the 1840s to the *Laborem Exercens* encyclical of Pope John Paul II in 1981. Along with changes in the economic needs of society, this desire becomes the impetus for formation of modern professions. In the long and sordid history of human labor, the concept of a profession, of being a professional, is relatively new. The expansion of this concept as a category of labor has increased dramatically over the past seventy years and is still in development. In many ways, the unique and emerging notion of "being a professional" is a dynamic concept rather than a static definition. The advent of modern professions is, at least in part, an attempt to actualize the hope and desire of improving the nature of work and thereby the value of work.

Professional Life and the Value of Work

What does it mean to be a "professional?" Four general criteria indicate a profession and typify the persons who occupy the roles therein: specific training, autonomy, public service, and ethical codes. First, most professions require some form of specific training, which may include specialized college degrees, apprenticeships, or licensing from a government or regulatory institution. Second, unlike other forms of employment, professions offer autonomy and give individual workers the freedom and independence to pursue the fulfillment of their work. Third, professions typically provide some variation of public service and may encourage its members to serve populations outside of the realm of the profession and to be committed to and involved in the community. Fourth, professions are also characterized by the creation of and adherence to ethical codes, which are unique to each vocation and which apply to their respective members. It is the last criterion, the formation and application of professional codes of ethics, on which the analysis of work and values in this book will focus.

Professional life offers the hope of rewarding work, not just financially but work that is fulfilling. Although the additional levels of education and specialized training can be difficult, people are willing to submit to such challenges out of desire and hope that the professions they enter will provide an opportunity for self-actualization rather than a mere means of survival. This is undoubtedly one feature which attracts people to professions over other jobs. However, professions are also riddled with complexities and recalcitrant aspects that obfuscate and impede the goal of meaningful work. The emergence of ethical dilemmas in the workplace is one of the most formidable problems which arises in a profession; it is one of the chief reasons for a great variety of professions to adopt unique and authoritative codes of ethics. Following through with the implementation of values articulated in the code would be a difficult enough endeavor in itself, without a further problem arising: the potential for conflicts between the profession's code and the personal moral beliefs and commitments of the profession's members.

This book is an exploration of these moral difficulties and of one possible, though seldom recognized, response to the contradictions and frustrations of professional life. After identifying the theoretical and philosophical suppositions that provide the foundation and structure of professional ethics, attention will turn to contemporary challenges in professional morality, especially the practical challenges that confront professionals on a daily basis. Throughout this analysis, however, I want to address these issues with responses and insights influenced by the life and writings of Thomas Merton, a Catholic monk in the Order of Cistercians of the Strictest Observance (Trappist) tradition, who wrote extensively on spiritual and social issues. He has been called "a spiritual master" for contemporary times.[1] Since his death in 1968, Merton's influence has not waned. In fact, it has increased dramatically in both spiritual and academic circles. Some of Merton's ideas are especially insightful when applied to social issues, such as the ordinary difficulties and hopes of professional life. His book, *Conjectures of a Guilty Bystander*, published in 1966, will be the primary text through which this analysis of professional and personal ethics will be illuminated.

Introduction to Thomas Merton

A brief introduction to the life of Thomas Merton may help to explain my belief in his relevance to issues of "the value of work." Thomas

Merton was born in 1915. Following the death of his mother at age five, he grew up in both Europe and America, being shuffled by his artist father between relatives and family friends. He became orphaned at the age of fifteen with the death of his father. After spending a tumultuous freshman year at Cambridge his guardian suggested that he attend Columbia University, which he did beginning in 1935, where, in addition to his studies, he wrote for a campus humor magazine. Gradually his life settled down, and he began to express an interest in religion. His life changed dramatically when he converted to Catholicism in 1938. He completed a master's degree in English at Columbia, accepted a teaching position at St. Bonaventure University in upstate New York, and began to consider entering the priesthood. In 1941, on the advice of an instructor at Columbia, Merton attended a spiritual retreat at the Trappist monastery of Our Lady of Gethsemani near Bardstown, Kentucky. A few months later, he joined the Order of Cistercians to pursue a contemplative life. Although he may have believed that he had renounced the world and the spoken word, he did not renounce the written word. The autobiographical account of his spiritual journey, *The Seven Storey Mountain*, was published in 1948 and became a bestseller. During the early 1950s, Merton became famous, as did the monastery. He published subsequent books during this period, including *The Bread of Life*, *The Sign of Jonas*, and *No Man Is an Island*. During this time he also was appointed Master of Scholastics at the monastery, the director of students preparing for the priesthood.

In the late 1950s, however, Merton's attitudes toward isolation and contemplation began to shift. His pursuit of the contemplative life became less about the purity of prayer and personal devotion and more about cultivating a deep inner spirituality from which one could critically encounter the world. By the early 1960s, Merton had become very outspoken about war, nuclear weapons, and racial issues in the United States. Contemplation became a springboard from which Merton could take an expansive view of issues and apply spiritual responses to them. The disengaged, world-denying monk of *Seven Storey Mountain* became a hermit engaging the world with compassionate criticism. This shift in his outlook and spiritual journey can be detected from the very titles of his books, in which a blatant semantic change occurs from earlier works to later works: from *Ascent to Truth* (1951) to *Emblems of a Season of Fury* (1963); *Seeds of Contemplation* (1949) to *Seeds of Destruction* (1964); from *The Silent Life* (1957) to *Raids on the Unspeakable* (1966). Within this last work, the most remarkable semantic shift occurs. In *Raids on the Unspeakable*, Merton publishes an essay from 1958 entitled, "Letter to an Innocent Bystander," which would soon starkly contrast the title of another book published later in 1966, which bore the provocative title, *Conjectures of a Guilty Bystander*, the object of this study.

Within "Letter to an Innocent Bystander" Merton explains the notion of bystanding and rejects the argument that one can remain honorable while being a "helpless witness" to appalling conditions. Merton asserts that one cannot be a detached observer while maintaining one's innocence. It is a mistaken belief, according to Merton, that innocence relieves one of responsibility. Even helpless witnesses can be "helpless" through their own neglect. Like the passersby in the infamous Genovese murder (a 1964 case of domestic violence in New York City in which witnesses of the event took no action to save the victim), people want to ignore circumstances and continue on about their business as if they were not affected by events or because they are waiting for others to take action.[2] However, Merton equates this sort of passive indifference with actively preparing one's own demise, practicing a "logic of failure" rooted in the comfortableness of evasion. Thus, bystanding is founded on an ethic of egoism, a desire to be uninvolved, to be "clean" and not dirtied by situations. Contrary to vulgar forms of moral self-interest, Merton asserts that standing up and speaking out requires community and the support of others; isolation and separation lead to conformity and silence.

It is interesting to note that Merton's "Letter to an Innocent Bystander" was also written in the same year as his epiphany on a street corner in downtown Louisville, Kentucky. Merton describes that event vividly in *Conjectures of a Guilty Bystander*:

> In Louisville, at the corner of Fourth and Walnut, in the center of the shopping district, I was suddenly overwhelmed with the realization that I loved all those people, that they were mine and I theirs, that we could not be alien to one another even though we were total strangers. It was like waking from a dream of separateness, of spurious self isolation in a special world, the world of renunciation and supposed holiness. . . . Though "out of the world" we [monks] are in the same world as everybody else, the world of the bomb, the world of race hatred, the world of technology, the world of mass media, big business, revolution, and all the rest. We take a different attitude to all these things, for we belong to God. Yet so does everybody else belong to God. We just happen to be conscious of it, and to make a profession out of this consciousness. . . . A member of the human race! To think that such a commonplace realization should suddenly seem like news that one holds the winning ticket in a cosmic sweepstake. . . . As if the sorrows and stupidities of the human condition could overwhelm me, now I realize what we all are. And if only everybody could realize this! But it cannot be explained. There is no way of telling people that they are all walking around shining like the sun.[3]

The book's title alone is indicative of the further shift in Merton's thought, for in this journal of personal reflections he now more deeply questions the "innocence" of bystanding and personal responsibility. The answer, which he relates in personal correspondence, is to "be responsible to everybody, to take upon oneself all the guilt."[4] Merton had come to the realization, in the words of Paul Pearson, "innocent bystanding was no longer possible—just to bystand made a person guilty because they were a part of the human race and therefore deeply implicated."[5] But what other alternative is there? How should a person make moral choices or act in a complex world with competing values, in which innocent bystanding is not possible but where we are all guilty? Merton's response in *Conjectures of a Guilty Bystander* is both autobiographical and prescriptive for all of us: "you must be willing, if necessary, to become a disturbing and therefore an undesired person, one who is not wanted because he upsets the general dream."[6]

This book is an attempt to "upset the general dream." It is an examination of moral values and how those values are expressed—or repressed—in professional life. It is not so much an effort to be disturbing or undesirable, but to make an appeal that Merton's call to contemplation can be a constructive force in the context of moral dilemmas encountered in our work lives on a daily basis. Perhaps this book will be disturbing to the extent that it points to ways in which our lives are shaped by institutional and organizational forces or that it examines weaknesses in professional codes of ethics and their application. Yet, the message here is a positive one: the contemplative perspective that Merton represents can enlighten and revive our commitment to making work meaningful—not just making a living but making a life worth living.

Two Controversial Claims

In order to commence straightaway with upsetting the general dream, I want to defend two somewhat controversial claims and demonstrate the connection between them. The first claim, which I have already introduced, is that Merton's work is relevant to issues of professional morality. Much of what Merton has to say, particularly in *Conjectures of a Guilty Bystander,* is applicable to the daily life of work. The second claim, more philosophical and no less debatable, is that language structures the way we experience the world.

Regarding the first claim, reflecting and writing on Thomas Merton's significance for professional life is not an altogether easy task, for in attempting to do it one has to recognize that the effort is akin to the old logic puzzle of an irresistible force meeting an immovable object. There are two things that, particularly by the time of his later writings, Merton has contempt for: politics and business. In an eloquent but sarcastic passage from *Conjectures*, Merton describes businesses as "quasi-religious sects."[7] He compares working in a business organization to embracing a new religious faith. Everything, including one's life, revolves around glorification of the product, communion with and ultimate submission to it. He even draws an analogy between the monastery and a place of business (he specifically mentions the GE plant in nearby Louisville, Kentucky; but it could be just as easily any office building, superstore or shop at any mall). Merton asks, "Which one is the more religious?" Using another analogy Merton concludes, "the religious seriousness of the monastery is like sandlot baseball compared with the big-league seriousness of General Electric." Hence, I realize that the attempt to draw a positive association between the business of professions and the insights of Thomas Merton might be a tenuous one. For devoted readers of Merton who find spiritual edification in his writings, this project may seem to be an altogether misguided one. Like trying to mix oil and water, some people may view an effort to bring together issues in professional ethics with the contemplative vision of Merton to be ultimately futile and marginally negligent of the nature of each ingredient.

While I have respect for this objection, even some sympathy for this point of view, I disagree with this perspective for several reasons. First, there is without question a "turning toward the world" which is present in Merton's writings, beginning in the late 1950s and certainly into the mid-1960s, which is the time period of the central text for this project, *Conjectures of a Guilty Bystander*. After his epiphany in the heart of downtown, surrounded by businesses and the bustle of hurried workers, the world-denying monk begins to engage the world rather than retreat from it. His interaction with the world takes the form of dialogue, not simply criticisms and condemnation from a lofty mountaintop. In Bill Murray's film adaptation of Somerset Maugham's novel, *The Razor's Edge*, the enlightened Murray decides to leave the isolated Himalayan temple in order to return to city-life and his former friends. When the Buddhist priest asks for an explanation of his departure, Murray wisecracks, "It is easy to be a holy man in the mountains."[8] It seems to me that Merton adopts a similar attitude: though he never abandons the monastery nor monastic life—quite the contrary, during this time of the mid-1960s he obtains permission to live as a hermit—his contemplative commitment serves as a foundation from which he can embrace the world in all of its beauty and contradiction. Merton reflects on the nature of truth in *Conjectures* and argues that dialogue is a surer way to truth than refutation. The task, he argues, is not to show how others are mistaken in their views but to recognize the truth in another's experiences and perspectives, then to show a higher truth beyond them.[9] This is Merton's attitude toward interfaith dialogue and it is, in part at least, what it means to act "in the spirit of Thomas Merton." Given his own analogy between the monastery and the business institution, my intention is to engage in a kind of interfaith dialogue, in the spirit of Thomas Merton, between professional ethics and commitment to a contemplative, spiritual approach to life.

A second reason that I disagree with objections to applying Merton's insights to moral issues in professions: I believe this connection between professional ethics and Merton is justifiable because membership in a profession, as such, has a different quality than mere participation in a business enterprise. This is due to the very nature of professions. One of the features of a profession is dedication and service to the community, to the common good. This is not to deny that business enterprises in general may also contribute, as Adam Smith would surely affirm. However, business in general may benefit as well, perhaps more, from the implications of Merton's insights. During these troubled times people in all walks of life, especially professions, are searching for paths to integrate their spirituality and values into their experiences of work. Professions in particular, because they are both implicitly and explicitly committed to human well-being, struggle with the ideals and pursuit of excellence in conflict with organizational roles and institutional demands. I believe that the words and spirit of Merton can speak to these pressing needs.

Regarding the second claim, without digging into the quagmire of contemporary theories of meaning or postmodern critiques of them, it is possible to show how one's understanding of reality and life is shaped by language. Traditional theories of language hold that words have *meanings*, composed primarily of lexical definitions which determine the proper use of a term. Postmodern theories, however, hold that words do not have fixed meanings, rather *usages* which are constantly in flux. The postmodern view asserts that we manipulate language to convey a variety of meanings in different contexts. Some scholars have even argued that without language, thought itself is not possible; one might have sensations and feelings, but ideas about them and reflections on them are not possible without language. So, my second arguably controversial claim is that language structures our experience.

A few examples might help to illustrate this point. For several years I taught a graduate bioethics course in a university extension program a few hundred miles from our main campus. As I traveled this route, over the course of time, something fascinating occurred to me: there are very few "truckstops" anymore. To be sure, these roadside depots still exist, but the proprietors do not call them truckstops any longer. Think of what imagery the term conjures up, a place where burly guys eat greasy food and tell off-color jokes, a place where typically only truck drivers would stop. But they aren't called truckstops any longer, today they are "travel plazas." These places are mini shopping malls, with food courts of several vendors and an assortment of merchandise from electronics to clothes, great places to spend the day with the whole family! Similarly, at the current moment there is a global economic crisis, but some politicians in the United States painstakingly avoid using the "R-word." Rather than recession they prefer to speak of "a meaningful downturn in economic activity." With ethical issues too: lying on a job application is unethical and grounds for immediate dismissal from many positions (the cases of George O'Leary or Marilee Jones are instructive), so management institutes and self-help gurus call it "resume enhancement" instead.[10] The concept of "global warming" sounds menacing, as though we must radically change our habits of consumption in order to save the planet and our very lives; but "climate change" sounds much less threatening and even inviting in the dead of winter. Of course these terms have political cachet as well, though many people (and surprisingly, even journalists) will use both of these phrases interchangeably. In fact, a 2006 *TIME* magazine article cites a Republican campaign advisor who attributes their campaign losses that year to "linguistic sloppiness."[11] Common people are more likely to rally around the issue of a "death tax" than to be concerned about the affluent-sounding "estate tax;" more likely to vote in favor of "free market" economic policies than over concerns of "globalization." Comedian George Carlin pointed out that we often put similar words together to make things sound better than they really are: free gift, money-back refund, added bonus, future plans, and other redundancies. Of course oxymorons are popular too: jumbo shrimp, new tradition, and my students' favorite, "business ethics." Your car may have an airbag, but mine has an "impact management system"—now in which one would you rather be riding? Other universities may have libraries, but ours has a "learning resource center." My favorite example from George Carlin: he claimed there is no such thing as an accident, it is "premeditated carelessness."

Business and professional life is replete with examples. When a large retailer decided to save money by eliminating its highest paid salespersons, the company referred to the plan as a "wage management initiative." The employees were "separated" from their jobs. "Fired" sounds too harsh. In fact, think of all the euphemisms for it: administrative leave, career change, dehired, downsized, early retirement, furloughed, given notice, pink slip, reduced, released, terminated; the list could go on. People tend to downplay purchases of expensive items by saying, "I *invested* in" a computer, a flat-screen TV, etc. An item isn't "used," it is "pre-owned." A clerk is a "customer representative," a secretary is an "administrative assistant," a cleaner or maid is a "domestic engineer," a dog catcher is a "canine relocation specialist," and a window washer is a "vision clearance engineer."

Language structures our experience because language has power. These are not simply euphemisms. There are core serious beliefs and values which mark the different usages of these phrases. The choice of a word or phrase, it's resonance within us, is a matter of the power which language has to convey our most deeply held beliefs. Ludwig Wittgenstein, a famous twentieth-century philosopher, is noted for saying, "The limits of my language are the limits of my world."[12] Language is not morally neutral, the words we use depict our beliefs and values about the world in which we live.

It may come as a surprise to even devout Merton readers, to realize that he shared this recognition of the importance of language. Merton's *Conjectures of a Guilty Bystander*, particularly the early sections, is replete with observations on the importance of language. Merton even suggests that language reflects our understanding and interpretation of experiences. He mentions a faux pas, a syntactical mistake, of a Kentucky governor who visited Gethsemani monastery during Merton's time there. The governor said, "You monks know that you cannot be happy because you have material possessions." Afterwards Merton pointed out the ambiguity of this statement to the novices. Strictly interpreted, the statement means that the monks are in despair because of their great possessions. But this is not, of course, what the governor meant. He intended to say something to the effect that, monks realize that possessions cannot make people really happy. Merton quips, "everyone instinctively pays attention not to what a politician actually says, but to what he seems to want to say."[13] The philosophical theorists who asserted that language has fixed meanings espoused a position known as Logical Positivism, and Merton explicitly comments on its merits, referring to it as a "mechanical clicking of the thought machine manufacturing nothing . . . about nothing," and summarizing its perspective in the idea that, "Since we cannot really say anything about anything, let us be content to talk about the way in which we say nothing." Merton adds, "That is an excellent way to organize futility."[14] Merton even comments on the way in which we use language when he observes that a reader in the refectory, a "particularly serious" person who is reading passages from *A Right to be Merry*, lowers his voice on the word "merry" as if to question a monk's right to use the word, but resoundingly emphasizes words like "death" and "dead" from the reading, "with utter finality," Merton says.[15]

Merton's astute observations about language are particularly evident in his criticisms of propaganda and political rhetoric. In one passage from *Conjectures of a Guilty Bystander*, Merton mocks quotations from Nazi concentration camp workers who documented braggingly, "We built our gas chambers to accommodate 2000 people at a time." Merton scoffs at the use of "accommodation," which implies "to make people comfortable." For Merton these linguistic constructions are not accidental but indicative of double-talk which is "systematically dedicated to an ambiguous concept of reality."[16] In another passage, he states his averseness for slogans, using rhetorical flourish to pressure people, to get others to serve one's own purposes; for Merton this is too intrusive on another's freedom.[17]

Some of Merton's most insightful comments on language focus on the concept of "contempt for the world," the renunciation of the reality of "this world" for the importance of the metaphysical, spiritual world assumed to be the higher reality. Over and again Merton addresses this pervasive religious dichotomy, rejecting traditional interpretations of its significance. He asks, "What do you mean by 'the world' anyway?" Moving away from theoretical abstractions, Merton offers his concrete answer: "What I abandoned when I left 'the world' and came to the monastery was the *understanding of myself* that I had developed in the context of civil society—my identification with what appeared to me to be its aims."[18] The significance of this statement should not be underestimated for those of us committed to both the pursuit of a deeper spiritual life and an active career. Merton exhibits a keen sense of self-understanding when he continues his explanation with the observation that, by this abandonment he did not necessarily mean any ambition to be successful or achieve personal goals, but he did mean rejection of "a certain set of servitudes that I could no longer accept—servitudes to certain standards of value which to me were idiotic and repugnant."[19] The implications for professional ethics of Merton's rejection of servitudes to particular standards of values needs further elaboration, but this passage is indicative of both his recognition of the power of language to structure our experiences and of his own self-understanding, both of which result from his devotion to contemplative practice.

In light of these two claims, that Merton's ideas, particularly from *Conjectures of a Guilty Bystander*, are relevant to professional life and that "language structures our experience of the world," we can now turn to an examination of the foundation and structure of professional ethics. Interestingly, some of Merton's observations are applicable to even some of the theoretical and philosophical perspectives which contribute to the formation of professional ethics.

CHAPTER TWO

MORAL THEORY AND PROFESSIONAL LIFE

Moral theory is not something that many people find useful in everyday life. Theory, by its very nature, seems detached and somewhat irrelevant to practical decision-making. Hence, many people probably suspect that moral theory is something for academics to argue about: interesting for philosophers, psychologists and sociologists, but of little use for the average person. From this point of view moral theory is, at best, a generalization about ordinary values and practical situations. But this view is overstated, because the relevance of moral theories to our everyday decision-making can, in fact, be demonstrated. In the same way that Thomas Merton speaks of "disposing of the myth that spirituality is not practical," in *Conjectures of a Guilty Bystander*, one may also attempt to address the challenge that moral theory is not practical.[1]

Any theory, from political to mathematical, can be seen as a broad generalization of principles and concepts that constitute a particular field. Hence ethical theories, with all of their variety, purport to articulate some of the basic values that human beings hold dear and to provide some insight into concepts which inform our moral deliberations. Of course, human beings have many values and those values are not always compatible with one another; moreover, it is often not clear, even to our own selves, which values are motivating our choices. So again, ethical theory can be insightful and informative as it helps to identify the principles on which we are acting and may also help us to clarify competing values when they come into conflict.

There are many theories of ethics. Some moral theories differ dramatically from others. Some theories seem quite esoteric, while others border on pop psychology. What distinguishes the theories from one another is typically the identification of a particular value as foundational to our deliberations over moral choices. The theories are relevant to practical life insofar as they highlight specific fundamental values and demonstrate the centrality of a given principle to our decisions. Furthermore, the theories also provide us with language, concepts, and meanings which we use to articulate reasons and justifications for our choices. Each theory has its own particular strengths and weaknesses. Although philosophical discussions of ethics date back to the time of Plato and Aristotle, it was not until the seventeenth century that the Enlightenment philosophers undertook the task of developing a systematic approach to ethical theory. Many of these philosophers, including Plato and Aristotle, understood themselves to be inquiring into the very structure of human nature, and articulating the essence of human nature and values in their theories. However, because many of the theories differ so greatly, it is an open question as to whether or not these theories express basic human nature. Moreover, as postmodernism asserts, it remains an open question as to whether or not there is any such thing as "basic human nature." Regardless of the status of a theory relative to human nature, the theories do provide us with a way of organizing our beliefs and attitudes. Additionally, (as just mentioned), the theories supply us with systematic justifications of our moral rules, and a language through which we can articulate our values and provide supporting reasons and justifications for those values. Moreover, moral theories also provide us with a variety of means by which to prioritize our principles and values, and assist us in clarifying the reasons for our choices, especially when we are confronted by conflicting values. So, setting aside issues of the status of moral theories, discussing moral theories is valuable, even for non-philosophers, because doing so makes us sensitive to the full array of moral reasons which we apply to particular situations.

Four Popular Theories of Ethics

For our purpose it is not necessary to examine a vast number of ethical theories, but it is important to focus on four major ones: virtue ethics, egoism, utilitarianism, and deontology. Some general consideration of each one of these theories will assist us in realizing the ways in which people have contemplated values.

Versions of virtue ethics date back to the time of Plato and Aristotle. For Plato, moral values are rooted in the very nature of the human soul. Plato has a relatively positive view of human nature. He believes that we are basically born good, but that the pressures and temptations of day-to-day life (particularly over-concern with our physical well-being and desire for pleasure) distract us from the best kind of human life and lead to the corruption of our souls. It is a positive view of human nature because Plato believed that deep down, inside ourselves, we have a sense of what is good and of what goodness requires. Interestingly for Plato, this sense of the good is also rooted in our communal life. For Plato, the community is "the individual writ large," the order and sensibility of a community is a reflection of the ordered and reasonable lives of its inhabitants. In other words, for Plato, morality is not simply a question of our own individual preferences or desires, but is reflected in the community of which we are a part, just as the community is a reflection of the nature of the collective souls which constitute it. Thus, Plato believes that we have an innate sense of "the Good," and that good is connected to the good of the community. But when we become overly concerned with our own prosperity or desires, our sense of the good becomes distorted, and the entire community suffers. Nevertheless, we can recover that awareness of goodness through Socratic contemplation and dialectic.

Aristotle's view shares much in common with Plato's perspective, yet with some important differences. For Aristotle, something is "good," when it fulfills its characteristic activity. That is, you know that something is a good X, when that thing does X things well. His classic example is that of a knife: the purpose of a knife, its characteristic activity, is to cut. So, one knows that one has a "good" knife when that object cuts things well. Having a beautiful handle or special etching along the blade may be nice, but these are not sufficient to make that a good knife. The key question, then, from Aristotle's perspective, becomes: what is the characteristic activity of human beings? Aristotle's answer is, reason. The ability to reason, to critically reflect, is for Aristotle the characteristic activity of a human being. Thus for Aristotle, a good human being is a person that reasons well.

But what does it mean to "reason well?" Is a person good if they merely show exceptional skill at rhetoric, mathematics, or logic problems? How does reason function to lead us to the good? For Aristotle, virtue is destroyed by either an excess or by a lack of particular traits. In other words, we can know that X is a virtue if X occupies a middle ground between two extremes. This belief is sometimes called Aristotle's doctrine of "the golden mean." We can know, claims Aristotle, that courage is a virtue because it occupies a middle ground between two extremes: a lack of courage, cowardice, on one side; and an excess of courage, foolhardiness, on the other extreme. Contemplating these values, critically reflecting on their importance, is for Aristotle the key to living a virtuous life.

It is also noteworthy that for Aristotle we must habituate ourselves to do good. Aristotle would agree with a slogan sometimes found in gyms and weight-rooms: "It is hard to do a great thing suddenly." He does not see the formation of habits in a negative way, rather he sees them in a positive light: using reason, we must train ourselves to act virtuously in difficult situations. Establishing good habits is, according to Aristotle, the development of character—much like the ability to lift heavy weights begins by training with lighter ones.

Egoism is another theory of ethics, periodically quite popular in Western culture, which asserts that the individual (or self) is the most important moral value. This is oftentimes the default moral position of many college undergraduates, and it is widely portrayed in movies and television shows. There is a "pop culture" or vulgarized view of egoism, and there is a more sophisticated version of it. The pop culture or vulgarized view is descriptive; that is, it simply describes how human beings behave. The more elaborate point of view is normative; which is to say, it attempts to articulate how human beings ought to behave.

The vulgarized or popular cultural perspective is often known as psychological egoism. It is sometimes associated with seventeenth-century philosopher, Thomas Hobbes. His view is descriptive, because he takes himself to be simply describing how, in fact, human beings behave; and, as described earlier, he takes himself to be articulating basic human nature.[2] Hobbes' view is that each person is constituted so as to look out for his or her own interests. We can't help it, it is just the way we are psychologically "hard-wired," to use a computer metaphor. Hence, from this perspective, although other people and moral theories may call for us to behave unselfishly, it is in fact contrary to our very nature to do so. The psychological make-up of each person is that he or she is oriented to act out of self-interest.

Now a person might believe, "Of course people sometimes act unselfishly," so this theory seems to fly in the face of facts. Note however that this theory relies on a strategy of re-interpreting motives. In other words, if we take any apparently altruistic act, deep down there is a self-interested motive guiding the action. Psychological egoism does argue that, human nature being what it is, people will only respond to the needs of others when there is something in it for themselves. Sometimes it may seem as though the only reward for a charitable act is a "good feeling" for the doer, but Hobbes would argue that we should not underestimate this motive. Whenever I do something for others, according to Hobbes, I get the good feeling precisely because I am exercising and asserting my power over others. So, when I give a few dollars to the panhandler on the street, the "good feeling" I experience comes from my demonstration (both to that person and to myself) that I am so in control of my own circumstances, I can provide for others without experiencing any loss on my own part. Hence, psychological egoism asserts that for any apparently charitable act a way can be found to reinterpret motives, such that the altruistic motive can be pushed aside for a more self-centered one.

In contrast to psychological egoism, "ethical egoism" is a normative view. This theory claims that, regardless of what one construes human nature to be, human beings *ought* to act in a self-interested manner. Sometimes this view is called "objectivism," and it is often associated with the philosophy of Ayn Rand. In some of her writings, she argues that selfishness is not a negative moral value. Look up the word "selfish" in the dictionary, Rand argues, and one will find a definition like: "concern with one's own interests." Rand asks, what is morally negative about this definition? Though we often associate the word selfish with a morally negative connotation, according to Rand there is nothing morally negative about concern for one's own interests. Hence, no matter what one takes human nature to be, ethical egoism maintains that human beings ought to be concerned with their own self-interests. In doing so everyone will be better off, because I will be taking care of my own interests and you will take care of your own interests.

It is important to note that the view of egoism develops largely in the post-Enlightenment period, and that no ancient philosopher would have defended the kind of radical individualism that most people in Western culture take for granted every day. Ethical egoism is often associated with libertarianism, not in the political sense, but not wholly different from it. As we will see, Merton has much to say about the radical individualism of contemporary society.

Utilitarianism and deontology are the two most prominent ethical theories in Western civilization, the influences of the previously mentioned theories notwithstanding. Both proponents of these theories (Jeremy Bentham for utilitarianism, Immanuel Kant for deontology) believe themselves to be articulating the basic structure of human nature and of moral decision-making. Despite the fact that each of these moral traditions take themselves to be providing the fundamental principle of morality, they are indeed quite different and sometimes posited as antithetical to each other.

Utilitarianism can best be summarized as, "the greatest good for the greatest number." One of its foremost proponents, Jeremy Bentham, characterized utilitarianism as the calculating of consequences in order to maximize happiness. Bentham argued that it was possible to develop a "hedonic calculus" by which we could mathematically calculate our moral preferences, based on the probability of several criteria to produce pleasure or pain. Bentham believed that it was basic human nature to consider the following seven criteria when evaluating a moral decision:

1. Intensity: How much pleasure do I believe that I will gain from this action?
2. Duration: How long is this pleasure or happiness expected to last?
3. Certainty or uncertainty: How sure am I that, on completion of my action, I will receive the expected happiness?
4. Propinquity or remoteness: How long must I wait for my action to come to fruition? One can see how criteria three and four work together: the farther out into the future that I expect results, generally speaking, the less certain I can be to receive the rewards of my action. Criteria five and six work together in much the same way as criteria three and four.
5. Fecundity: By "fecundity," Bentham means, what are the chances that by pursuing this happiness I may incur other pleasures of a similar kind?
6. Purity: By "purity," Bentham means, what are the chances that by pursuing this happiness I may incur sensations of an opposite kind? Now each of these questions could be answered from an individual's point of view. But Bentham supposed that we do not address these issues as radical individualists. Thus,
7. Extent: We take into account the "extent" to which our choices and actions affect other people.

Bentham thought that we find it possible to quantify our responses to each of these questions, thereby developing a hedonic calculus, which results in each individual acting in accordance with the basic principle of calculating consequences in order to maximize happiness for the greatest number of people.

Contemporary utilitarians, like Peter Singer, perhaps the best-known living philosopher at this time, have been critical of Bentham's choice of happiness as the primary criterion of these seven categories. Utilitarians like Singer argue that we consider "preferences," not happiness, as the central value in our determinations of the greatest good for the greatest number. In his book, *Rethinking Life and Death*, Singer argues that older, traditional values such as "treat all human life as equal" need to be replaced by contemporary values such as the recognition that all human lives are not equal, and that we should replace the admonition to "never intentionally take innocent human life" with the present-day imperative to "take responsibility for our choices." Singer believes that these "new commandments" or moral principles can provide better guidance for the ethical complexities of the twenty-first century. These new commandments, he claims, are more consistent with contemporary preferences.[3]

Deontology comes from a Greek root word which literally means, "doing what one is supposed to do." It is a theory that prescribes (versus describes, hence it is normative) what the fundamental duties of a person are. The ordinary terms in our language of morals like duty, responsibility, obligation, rights, etc., are placed on a different philosophical foundation in this theory. One of the foremost proponents of this theory, Immanuel Kant, perhaps the premier Enlightenment philosopher, argues that what is right is independent of any consequences or outcomes which we might expect from an action.[4] Hence for Kant, specific actions are right or wrong in and of themselves, regardless of the outcomes or consequences of the actions, in spite of one's circumstances, culture, race, religion, or socio-economic standing. Deontologists like Kant emphasize that an action should be deemed right or wrong based on one's motives, not the consequences of the action. For example, Kant's view supports the notion that breaking a promise is always wrong regardless of the circumstances.[5] Deontological theory emphasizes the importance of having good intentions, which is more important than simply a good outcome. In the writings of Kant, for example, this is why having self-respect is so important: a person with self-respect is likely to do the right thing in ambiguous situations and in face of strong temptations. Moral duty, doing what is right, is more important than even our legal obligations. Thus, Martin Luther King, Jr.'s persistence in efforts to challenge our sense of justice and equality, even though arrested many times, is morally justifiable from a deontological point of view. Conversely, by deontological standards a person has a duty to obey the law even if no one is watching; for example, even when there is no possibility of being caught, a person has a duty to obey the laws of traffic.

Deontological ethics emphasizes the point that the individual cannot be sacrificed for the greater good of the majority. But this need not commit us to a Randian egoism. By deontological lights, individuals have rights that are of supreme moral value and which should not be violated. Thus we arrive at a philosophical justification of "rights" such as the right to life, free speech, the right to control one's own body, to own private property, etc. These rights supersede the good of the majority, which separates deontology from utilitarianism on two grounds: One, actions can be evaluated morally apart from consideration of the consequences; and two, the individual is of greater moral importance than the collective. For deontologists like Kant, the fundamental principle of morality is, "act only on that maxim which you could, at the same time, will to be universal law." This principle of universalizability is the foundation of deontological theory. More recent theorists and psychologists, such as Lawrence

Kohlberg, argue that deontology represents the highest stage of human moral development.

These are four theories of ethics which attempt to lay the foundation and justifications for our moral choices. While there are other ethical theories that might also be considered (for example, I have not addressed religious versions of ethics) these theories represent some of the diversity and general popularity of moral perspectives. Arguably, these are some of the most persuasive theoretical perspectives. On occasion one may hear a person appeal to aspects of these four theories when defending an action or responding to that nagging question, "Why did you do that?"

Mertonesque Reflections on Theories of Ethics

Virtue theory emphasizes care of the soul and the development of good character. In *Conjectures of a Guilty Bystander*, Merton speaks about the "overstimulated society," in a way that is certainly consistent with Plato's perspective (with a hint of anti-utilitarianism too). Merton describes how having too many desires can take away one's peace of mind and keep one from finding genuine happiness. Similar to the view of Aristotle, Merton sees an inherent connection between virtue and happiness. The best kind of life for a human being is linked to a pursuit of goodness and excellence, and though this pursuit may take place from a variety of perspectives, goodness and excellence are neither relative nor subjective terms. In *Conjectures*, Merton affirms Plato's view that we degrade ourselves when we allow illusory goods to distract us from the goal of a virtuous life. Merton questions why we allow the standards of happiness to be defined by culture, particularly mass media, as if happiness were simply a matter of making the right purchases. There is a contradiction here, which Merton clearly exposes: Though magazines, TV, and now the internet may tout their capacity to sell us happiness, it is contrary to the nature of advertising and business for us to ever be truly content. The purchase of contentment would have a drastically negative effect on future sales! Yet, as members of affluent society, we seldom critically reflect on the way that these contextual forces influence our lives, values, and self-identities.[6]

Merton goes on to add that one of the things we seek most, indeed motivating much of our excessiveness, is the approval of others. There can be no doubt that the desire to be approved by others can motivate us to follow professional demands when the beacon of virtue points us in a different direction.

Egoism highlights the importance of the individual and places a high value on personal freedom. To some extent it is true that Merton focuses on the self, but he is clearly not a proponent of egoism. His analyses of ethical issues are normative, not simply descriptive. He actively draws us toward what could be, what should be the case, not a passive account of what simply is the case. Moreover, Merton emphasizes self-knowledge and understanding, not self-aggrandizement. His careful observations on the notion of "contempt for the world" provide the evidence. He soundly rejects the view of egoism and it's vulgar projection of the paramount importance of individual success and prosperity. He is particularly critical of the notion, so often present in "spiritualized" self-help and self-promotion perspectives, that one pursues the same interests as the world—private prosperity and self-enhancement—but from a different motive. Using the religious metaphor of "contempt for the world," he exposes the hypocrisy of holding in contempt not the ways of the world but one's fellow competitors for the same selfish ends. Merton argues in *Conjectures* that, too often, contempt for objectives motivated by base desires becomes not a rejection of those desires as such, but a disregard for one's like-minded contestants in trying to acquire them. Rather than challenging the worthiness of those desires, one simply holds in contempt others who also seek the same ends, believing in the superiority of one's motives over the motives of others. The opposition between "spiritual" and "secular" is a trivial one, more akin to the rivalry which exists between two automakers than anything more substantive. Ford and GM may have different strategies but they are in the same business; in Merton's words a "spirit of fraternal rivalry" exists between them. So it is, he reasons, between people who pursue self-promotion and personal success at the expense of others, believing that *their* motives (especially when attached to some "spiritual" appeal), separate and dignify *their* pursuit of the same worldly goals as others.[7]

Hence, for Merton the distinction between self and other is analogous to the dichotomy between industrial powers X and Y; indicative of his famous epiphany on a downtown street corner, Merton argues that a deeper unity underlies our shallow distinctions and selfish rivalries. Though Merton does indeed focus on the sense of self-identity and self-knowledge which he believes is necessary to a deeply fulfilling existence, his perspective does not support the position of the self as the most important moral value. On the contrary, Merton believes—especially after is his epiphany—that there is a fundamental human unity between oneself and others.

Utilitarianism stresses the consequences of one's actions, and most certainly provides philosophical foundation for much public policy. In *Conjectures of a Guilty Bystander*, Merton is very critical of some public policies of the time. However, sharing some of the same misgivings which Kant expressed, Merton is critical of acting on the basis of consequences, especially immediate consequences. When our deliberations become focused solely on what is practical and what is most efficient, we have turned our attention toward means, not ends. Over time, becoming habituated to this mode of ethical decision-making, we develop a myopic focus on immediate consequences. Merton argues,

> In this way we so completely lose all perspective and sense of values that we are no longer able to estimate correctly what even the most immediate consequences of our actions may turn out to be . . . we lose all capacity to grasp the significance of these reactions, and hence we cannot see further than the next automatic response. Having lost our ability to see life as a whole, to evaluate conduct as a whole, we no longer have any relevant context into which our actions are to be fitted, and therefore all our actions become erratic, arbitrary, and insignificant.[8]

Deontology downplays the consequences but focuses on motives, and lays the foundation for justification of concepts like rights and duties. Merton would seem to agree with Kant on some levels, but of course Merton points beyond Kant's deontological theory and indeed beyond any systematic approach to ethics. There are several reasons for this: first, Kant is not very good at telling us how to adjudicate between conflicting duties (though other deontologists like David Ross have attempted to overcome this weakness); second, Merton views blind allegiance to any system or authority in a suspect manner. Nietzsche claims, "the will to a system is a lack of integrity," and I believe that Merton would concur with that expression. More importantly, Merton advocates a law that is higher than a principle of universalizability, and that is the law of love. Merton states, "the law of love is the deepest law of our nature, not something extraneous and alien to our nature. Our nature itself inclines us to love, and to love freely."[9] Beyond glib recognition of another's dignity, deeper than an obligation to respect, Merton argues that we have a fundamental duty to love one another and that through love we fulfill our other moral obligations.

Ethical Theories and Professional Life

To be clear, I would not want to argue that anyone follows any one of these theories exclusively. Although I suspect that most of our moral decisions, particularly the difficult ones, are made on the basis of utilitarian or deontological grounds (with hints of egoism mixed in), I doubt that few if any people are devoted solely to one ethical perspective. I even doubt that to do so would be wise: A manager who makes decisions based on utilitarian grounds may be very good at calculating consequences and maximizing outcomes in particular situations, but might come across as being overly influenced by expediency and as unprincipled. Conversely, a manager beholden to a deontological framework might be very principled, always doing things "by the book," but may appear to decide matters very rigidly and to be cavalier about consequences. Moreover, it should be said that these theories do not, of themselves, take positions on ethical issues. Rather, we use these theories (their philosophical foundations and the language which they employ) to justify our positions on issues and to support our reasons for believing one way or another, often after the fact.

There can be no doubt that these theories, with the possible exception of some aspects of egoism, also provide the background and philosophical justification for a wide variety of professional ethics standards. We have been drawn toward these lines of work for various reasons: First, the notion of work as a "calling" and the belief that there is a "fit" between one's self-identity and the requirements of work. There is the idea, certainly evident in discussions of the Protestant work ethic, of work as a vocation; that is, the notion that there is an occupation that each person is particularly suited to or toward which one is naturally gifted. Second, the development of professions, the expansion of the professional sphere, attracts persons to it with its promise of a higher standard of living. Being a member of a profession is taken to entitle one to certain rights, privileges, and a steady, if not predictable, income. Third, we are drawn toward these occupations by the notion of a "noble profession," the idea that one is not only serving oneself but that one is dedicated to the service of others. Interestingly, several occupations now lay claim to this concept of being a "noble" profession, including lawyers, nurses, teachers, and more. The reason, I believe, is simple: we want work to be "good," not just for ourselves (in the fashion of the egoism) but also for others, indeed all of humanity; and we want work to be good not just in the sense of providing a good living, but work which makes life worth living—work which gives meaning to our lives. Hence, the fourth, we want work to be fulfilling, to contribute to our self-actualization and self-understanding.

Labor historian Daniel Rodgers has argued that there is an implicit connection between work and the moral life. Work makes one useful; it spares one from the temptations of idleness; it opens up the possibility of achieving wealth and social status; and it promotes the development of one's creativity and skill. But these aspects which link vocation and the "good life" also become points of dissatisfaction and resentment. With recent business trends like mergers, downsizings, early retirement packages, phase outs, and closures, employees are less likely to interact at their places of employment with confidence and trust. The focus changes to what is best for one's self, the ethic of egoism, and the "good life" becomes associated with leisure, not with the activity of work. Moreover, these recent trends contribute to an atmosphere in which neither having the appropriate degree nor possessing an abundance of related experience is sufficient for acquiring a desired position, much less for being guaranteed a successful career in that profession. Hence the meaning of work becomes "all about me," we all become independent contractors of a sort. Then, as isolated individuals, we are no match for the ethical dilemmas and moral slippery slopes foisted on us—the pressure of conformity is too great.

So this is where the tension mounts, for when we take on one of these professional roles we do so in the context of our own private moral beliefs and commitments. Inevitably there are times when our personal moral beliefs will conflict with the responsibilities of our profession, perhaps even values articulated in its code of ethics. This is the basis for the distinction between *personal* morality and *professional* morality; what one approves privately may be prohibited professionally, and vice versa. This phenomenon has also been called "role morality," for the tendency to take on the morality of one's assigned roles in life. Hence contemplation of values is very important and has been very useful through the development of these theoretical positions, which give us a language with which to discuss our values and also provide philosophical reasons and justifications (as opposed to mere opinions or assertions) to support our moral values and claims. And so here the value of contemplation becomes evident, as we critically reflect on the ethical values of our professions and the conflicts that arise in our occupation of professional roles.

Moral Life and Fragmentation of the Self

Many scholars and social critics would agree that relativism (another theory of morality which argues that all values are relative to one's culture) and postmodernism (the view that language, meanings and interpretations are subjective, not objective) are two of the most powerful challenges to Western culture and values at the beginning of the twenty-first century. As described in prophetic fashion by Allan Bloom in his popular and provocative book from thirty years ago, *The Closing of the American Mind*, much of the strength of both of these cultural influences is supported by the philosophy of Friedrich Nietzsche.[10] In the second part of his *Untimely Meditations*, "The Uses and Disadvantages of History for Life," Nietzsche argues that:

> It is possible to live almost without memory, and to live happily moreover, as [an] animal demonstrates, but it is altogether impossible to live at all without forgetting. Or to express my theme even more simply: there is a degree of . . . the historical sense, which is harmful and ultimately fatal to the living thing, whether this living thing be a man or a people or a culture.[11]

Nietzsche believes that the "historical" (the expression and examination of events of the past) and the "unhistorical" (a premeditated and deliberate forgetting of the past) are both necessary for the well-being of individuals and cultures:

> To determine this degree, and therewith the boundary at which the past has to be forgotten if it is not to become the gravedigger of the present, one would have to know exactly how great the *plastic power* of a man, a people, a culture is: I mean by plastic power the capacity to develop out of oneself in one's own way, to transform and incorporate into oneself what is past and foreign, to heal wounds, to replace what has been lost, to recreate broken moulds. There are people who possess so little of this power that they can perish from a single experience, from a single painful event, often and especially from a single subtle piece of injustice, like a man bleeding to death from a scratch.[12]

In contrast to Nietzsche's view, other social critics and commentators believe that as a culture we have erred in becoming far too "plastic," to use Nietzsche's term. Social conservatives and so-called communitarians claim that the pervasive relativism of current American society undermines the development of character and virtue. "Any attempt to envisage each human life as a whole, as a unity, whose character provides the virtues with an adequate *telos* (sense of purpose, linked to Aristotle's concept of "characteristic activity" discussed earlier) encounters two different kinds of obstacle," claims distinguished philosopher and noted author Alasdair MacIntyre in his insightful book, *After Virtue*:

[One sort of obstacle, social, is] . . . the way modernity partitions each human life into a variety of segments, each with its own norms and modes of behavior. So work is divided from leisure, private life from public, the corporate from the personal. [The second sort of obstacle, philosophical] . . . is the tendency to think atomistically about human action and to analyze complex actions and transactions in terms of simple components. [13]

For MacIntyre, the fragmentation of the individual self into a variety of roles that one occupies obscures the essential unity of a human life. The life of an individual becomes a disconnected series of episodes, with choices and actions evaluated merely by the relative moral codes of the various roles which one occupies at any given moment. The consequence, according to MacIntyre, is loss of a sense of wholeness to life—loss of unity and singularity of purpose and meaning—and thus the disappearance of virtue:

[T]he liquidation of the self into a set of demarcated areas of role-playing allows no scope for the exercise of dispositions which could be genuinely accounted virtues in any sense remotely Aristotelian . . . . What are spoken of as the virtues of a good committee man or of a good administrator or of a gambler or a pool hustler are professional skills professionally deployed in those situations where they can be effective, not virtues. [14]

This fragmentation of the self, which MacIntyre believes is endemic to modernity, results in a loss of the meaning of character. Today we are much more comfortable saying that someone "is a character" than claiming that someone is a "person of character," for there are no culturally agreed-upon standards which would rationally justify such a judgment. Humans who occupy a world without references for virtue or character lose sight of a sense of personal meaning and purpose. Then they lose a sense of wholeness.

This loss of wholeness would be felt by a person, underlying the activities and roles occupied by that person, and would certainly manifest itself in one's professional life. It leads to a distinction between ordinary morality and role morality, a separation between one's personal moral commitments and the values promoted by a particular role which a person might occupy. This problem will be discussed in greater detail later.

Thinking of the "story of my life"—developing what MacIntyre calls a "narrative sense of self"—provides a healing balm for the individual ripped apart by the fragmenting forces of modernity. He argues that the cure for this liquidation of the self into various roles lies in the concept of tradition; locating or situating oneself in a tradition restores a sense of wholeness and purposefulness to life and stands in stark contrast to the radical individualism of contemporary society:

> What I am, therefore, is in key part what I inherit, a specific past that is present to some degree in my present. I find myself part of a history and that is generally to say, whether I like it or not, whether I recognize it or not, one of the bearers of a tradition.[15]

Hence many people argue that a false and harmful perspective of self is promoted in our current liberal society. It is false because self-identity is gained from, and to some extent dependent on, our familial, communal, and social relationships and responsibilities. It is a harmful view of the self because claiming that we have freedom to choose these relations and responsibilities at will—even presupposing that we can be or are independent of them—erodes the value of responsibility and gives us an incorrect representation of our self-identity and self-worth. Without the cultural support and promotion of these elements, as Aristotle noted, society *and humanity* hardly seem possible.[16] Merton, too, is highly critical of radical egoism. "The heresy of individualism," he states in *Conjectures*, is "thinking oneself a completely self-sufficient unit and asserting this imaginary 'unity' against all others."[17] The concept of ethics itself presupposes relationships with others. (If you were marooned alone on an island, you might sin, but you wouldn't do anything unethical! Recall Tom Hanks in *Cast Away* and other variations on Robinson Crusoe).

A Holistic View of the Self

But is MacIntyre's case overstated? MacIntyre articulates a value, this *myth* of wholeness, which many social conservatives and communitarians hold, and he promotes it as a particular characteristic of historical consciousness. It is a characteristic or quality that is projected backward upon people of the past, and forward with hopeful expectation of recovering it; but it is claimed to be—to our detriment—lacking in the present.

Why refer to this belief as a "myth"? A myth can be defined as an imaginary story or matter used to explain some practice or phenomenon. People have long employed myths to support various activities, cultural beliefs, and to promote deeply held values. Sometimes myths are laudable in conveying a profound truth, sometimes myths obscure reality and distort the truth. Hence, it occasionally becomes beneficial to critique a myth and its influence over people's views. In *Conjectures* Merton states, "When a myth becomes a daydream it is judged, found wanting, and must be discarded. To cling to it when it has lost its creative function is to condemn oneself to mental illness."[18] Merton does not argue that we should attempt to live without myths (he calls this a dangerous idea) but he does argue that we should avoid truth-evading daydreams. He calls the belief that "America is the earthly paradise" the great myth of the United States, and he heavily criticizes this myth and the self-deception which follows from it. According to Merton the end of the American myth comes with the realization that Americans do not breathe the rarefied air of an ideal republic, but are just like others and are in the same mess as everyone else (indeed may be the cause of others' messes).

Therefore, at least two arguments support referring to the concept of the "wholeness of the self" as a myth. First, there are good reasons to believe that members of past generations did not enjoy the sort of holistic sense of self and purposefulness attributed to them by our contemporaries. Western history, on biographical and autobiographical accounts, is replete with examples of individuals struggling against the prevailing customs and cultures of their age and location, forging their sense of self-identity in relation to the communities of which they were a part. Second, I refer to it as the "myth" of wholeness because the unity of the self which is praised so highly lacks greater theoretical and conceptual clarity. This "wholeness" is ill-defined by scholars and social critics, primarily, one might suppose, because its presence is so lacking in our own time. Nevertheless, it is projected upon people of the past as inhabitors of a holistic perspective. It is projected upon the present and future, our future, as the lacking ingredient (or feasible solution) to contemporary intellectual and cultural crises. Moreover, it is imperative to recall Plato's characterization of society as "the individual writ large," and to consider the relationship between individual and social wholeness.

To the first issue, I have indicated some reservations as to whether or not past generations enjoyed such unified perspectives. It is true that the traditional philosophical canon has valued the writings of Plato over those of other philosophers of his time, and perhaps rightfully so. But to claim that his generation had a common world-view seems erroneous and trivializes the differences between Socrates and the Sophists. Moreover, Xenophon gives a different presentation of Socrates in his writings than does Plato. Is this simply a case of two authors giving different accounts of the same events and person? Consider the case of Aristotle, the energetic pupil of Plato who may have at least given Greeks the impression that theirs was a unified world-perspective: he often spends pages on differing and antithetical accounts of various topics, so much so that it is sometimes difficult to remember that he has yet to give his own view. Apparently his world was as lacking in wholeness as our own. Consider the fundamental tensions (antithetical to a unified worldview) between Augustine and the Manichaeans, or the Donatists, or the Pelagians. Aquinas lived and thought in the midst of very divergent perspectives and world-views. And recall the life and times of Martin Luther, who challenged Eck, Cajetan, and of course, Zwingli. Not to be overlooked in this regard is the contrarian John Calvin. Where is the cultural unity in his or any of these cases? Their world was just as fragmented and in flux as our world.

Secondly, I refer to this as a myth because it is poorly defined by communitarians and social critics and is at best paradoxical. To detect such wholeness in the lives of persons in the past, while proposing its absence in our own, would seem to require that we possess a higher level of cultural self-understanding than the very people we otherwise envy. Present generations apparently possess enough unity to recognize the higher virtues possessed by past generations, but lack enough judgment and critical self-understanding to be able to justify and reproduce them in the present. We simultaneously imagine ourselves to be superior and inferior on the same point, thus the basis for such a view is open to question.

Hence, underlying the diversity and pluralism of the current age there looms an assumption, again part of the belief in a privileged historical status, that other generations, unlike our own, have benefited from a shared world-view or tradition, which we as modern or postmodern "rootless cosmopolitans" no longer have. That is, we have, perhaps constructively, come to hold that people of the distant and not-too-distant past have participated in, stored, shared, and lived out of a commonly held unified perspective. The belief in this prior and expired unified perspective is the source of our contemporary myth of wholeness. Consider the claim of Ortega y Gassett:

> This inner duality and dissension between reason and faith is so habitual to us—to all of us, whether Catholics or irreligious—we are submerged in it in a fashion so inborn, that we do not perceive it very clearly. It is this that prevents us from placing ourselves in the position of the pure medieval man, the pure Christian whose life was at root unitary.[19]

Who or where is this "pure" medieval man, much less this "pure" Christian? Is it Augustine or Pelagius, Anselm or Abelard, Luther or Cajetan? Nevertheless, as I mentioned, many scholars and social critics assert or assume this sort of holistic self in their writings. Communitarians like Amitai Etzioni have echoed MacIntyre's yearning for a holistic view of the self. Contemporary critic Charles Taylor makes a similar point in a section on "Singularity" of his work, *Ethics of Authenticity*.[20] The myth finds expression in a variety of disciplines, and often in very subtle ways. It is evident in the last chapter of Auerbach's *Mimesis:*

> The widening of man's horizon, and the increase of his experiences, knowledge, ideas, and possible forms of existence, which began in the sixteenth century, continued through the nineteenth at an ever faster tempo—with such a tremendous acceleration since the beginning of the twentieth that synthetic and objective attempts at interpretation are produced and demolished every instant. The tremendous tempo of the changes proved the more confusing because they could not be surveyed as a whole. They occurred simultaneously in many separate departments of science, technology, and economics, with the result that no one—not even those who were leaders in the separate departments—could evaluate the resulting overall situations.[21]

Notice that Auerbach not only asserts the lack of a world-view possessed by other generations but also implies that we should be able to judge our own generation from the vantage of some future position at which we have not yet arrived. Auerbach also alludes to a generation that longs to name itself as a means of self-understanding. This reinforces the point, language structures the way in which we experience the world. We want to give ourselves a name, as if by naming we not only *identify* but also *control* and at least partially justify ourselves by virtue of our self-naming. "Baby Boomers," "Generation X," followed by "Generation Y" of course, then the "Millennium Generation." Trying to understand ourselves by naming ourselves is a fascination of recent generations.

These historical references illustrate that it seems presumptuous or pretentious to project onto the past a unity of thought or perspective that may not have existed. Likewise, it seems equally problematic to dogmatically assert a universal set of values or principles that might give a holistic sense of self to individuals of a particular generation. To do so would imply that, either issues are considered as being resolved that were in fact not resolved at that time, or else later generations such as ours choose a definitive stance which they inherit (or construct) and project that perspective backwards onto the past, obscuring diversity itself. To consider past generations benefactors of a unified view is merely to ascribe values to an alien culture of our own making. Nor would attributing a holistic perspective to individuals in the distant past appear to be particularly insightful or helpful for interpreting contemporary times.

An objection might be raised, however: "Even though a diversity existed, one world-view or perspective dominated others; one view had priority over others, and we lack anything comparable." This refined version of the claim has greater merit. In his later writings, particularly a section of *Three Rival Versions of Moral Inquiry* titled "Aftermath of a Defeated Tradition," MacIntyre seems receptive to this possibility. He alludes to what appears to be the real difficulty with our generation: what we lack is not a unified world-view, but *commitment*.[22] There is a reluctance on the part of individuals to commit to any tradition or perspective which might seem to encroach on one's personal freedom. In this age of non-commitment, *responsibility* is nearly a vulgar term. In *Conjectures*, Merton anticipates this observation when he claims that the "assertion of individuality as ultimate," leads to a false view of the radically free individual, who can select from several varieties and qualities of possible actions,

> no longer responsible to anyone . . . free to do exactly as he pleases without rendering an account to anyone and without taking into consideration the moral and physical consequences of any of his acts.[23]

Our world faces a variety of complex issues and problems—political environmental, educational, social, and economic—which, as members of this generation, we must not only acknowledge but address. No single principle or perspective will likely be the blade that cuts the Gordian knot, resolving all conflicts across a diverse spectrum. Cultural schemas (modernism, postmodernism, communitarian, etc.) come in as wide a variety as ethical theories—this is the point of recognizing and respecting diversity—but cultural criticism can still be utilized as a tool for resolving problems that we face. However, this cannot be done in its fullest sense as long as we have a nostalgic conception of a bygone holistic worldview or of an illusive wholeness of the present.

Hence, when we examine issues of professional ethics, when we confront tensions between personal morality and role morality, it seems of little use to appeal to bygone days of unified world-views or mythical holistic selves. Could there be such a thing as professional wholeness? If so, how should individuals in those occupations relate to it? Positing some interior unified self as the key to resolving complex moral dilemmas at work seems as much a daydream as the belief that America is an "earthly paradise," a view which Merton criticizes as a useless and harmful daydream. Rather, I believe the way to progress beyond this myth of wholeness is precisely how Merton suggests Americans should move beyond that myth: by realizing they are a part of everyone else in the world, just like everyone else. It is more useful and takes us a step further toward the truth, to explore Merton's conception of the unity of self, then to apply Merton's insights to problems in professional ethics.

Unity of Self with Others: Quest for Community

We have already noted Merton's argument against what he calls the heresy of individualism, and we have noted that for Merton unity of the self does not come through the juxtaposition of oneself against others, but it must rest on some other foundation. I have called this the myth of wholeness and have attempted to show why it is a poor starting point for the problems of professional ethics. Merton argues that whenever one seeks to affirm the unity of the self simply by negating the other, by denying any relationship to anyone else, in the end there is nothing left to affirm. Merton's suggestion leads in the opposite direction. "The more I am able to affirm others," Merton states, "by discovering them in myself and myself in them, the more real I am."[24] Throughout *Conjectures of a Guilty Bystander*, Merton argues that a genuine unity of the self is rooted in unity with others. Reminiscent of Jesus' claim that one finds oneself by losing oneself, Merton argues that when we empty ourselves, when we cast off the illusory self that has been constituted by our desires, fears and appearances for others, then we come closer to finding our authentic selves.[25] This is why Merton so forcefully rejects the perspective of egoism. Personal wholeness and self-unity cannot come through the glorification of individualism. To do so only results in, "an intellectual and moral blindness that comes from basing all truth and all law upon one's inner relation to oneself, and not upon one's relation to others."[26]

Moreover, Merton rejects the view that wholeness or unity of the self consists of an "inner peace" based on an interior relation to oneself. He refers to this view as disastrous, for it places the foundation for wholeness simply on the extent of one's self-approval. It is ruinous precisely because one may engage in bad actions which have no negative impact on one's psyche. This is particularly true in the area of professional ethics, for one might engage in dubious actions as a matter of course, and might daily and routinely commit harmful deeds, yet live in perfect peace with oneself.

Other moral theories also reject this idea of placing such a high importance on the self. For example, noted utilitarian philosopher Peter Singer has used the analogy of psychopathy to argue that meaning in life comes from finding purpose beyond our own self-interests. Singer claims that we must go beyond inward looking concerns and personal interests, toward the transcendent view of an impartial spectator, a perspective he refers to as "the point of view of the universe." Unfortunately it becomes very difficult for Singer to explain exactly what this position is or to elaborate on its nature.[27]

Merton's objections against utilitarianism notwithstanding, there may be some similarities between Singer's "point of view of the universe" and Merton's notion that unity of the self is rooted in unity with others. But with a different motive: not the greatest good for the greatest number, but love—an acceptance and charity toward one's fellow human beings that is manifest not only in belief but action. Merton is unique in his call for a metaphysical, spiritual recognition of unity that is not psychological, social, or political. In existentialist language, the unity to which Merton aspires aims at the heart of being. In *Conjectures*, he asserts that people myopically fail to see their deeper unity with God and with others when they become individually obsessed with their own inner unity,

> for it is in union with others that our own inner unity is naturally and easily established. To be preoccupied with achieving inner unity first and then going on to love others is to follow a logic of disruption which is contrary to life.[28]

What must be explored further, however, is how this unity of the self might manifest itself in professional life. An even more profound difference between Singer's point of view of the universe and Merton's notion of unity of the self through union with others may be evident here: the former can be (though not necessarily) detached and non-relational, while the latter implies relationship (though not necessarily a deep one). Anne Carr, who has most extensively written on Merton's conception of the self, argues that *Conjectures* represents a turning point in Merton's thought, a recognition of the inherent link between self and society. In her book, *A Search for Wisdom and Spirit*, she claims that Merton's notion of a false self is linked to "social myths created by mass media . . . crisis, fear, consumption, and competition."[29] However, the true, inner self is discovered through contemplation, not in a manner detached from the world but through critical reflection on the world as the self's natural environment. A person's inner unity or wholeness is inherently linked to one's relationships with others. Hence, one of the difficulties for professional ethics is to explicate how one's relationships with others might be morally problematic given the responsibilities of one's profession.

As discussed earlier, service to others is one of the fundamental characteristics of the profession. This feature of professions is not to be downplayed or undervalued, because often acting in the role of a professional means exercising power over others. But as Merton notes in *Conjectures*, powerful people do not rule by their power. Rather, power rules through people.[30] Persons in the legal and healthcare professions are admonished by their codes of ethics to provide some services *pro bono*; this is rooted not only in a concern for social justice but also in recognition that persons occupying these powerful roles can control the access, quantity, and quality of services which persons receive (particularly persons without adequate financial resources).

"Community" is a word which, philosophically, is notoriously difficult to define. Making the case for unity with others, as Merton does, seems to imply the concept of community in both some specific ways and in its broadest sense. There are all sorts of communities, and in attempting to define them one must first determine whether one is speaking about places or people. One could speak geographically of "the local community," the Louisville community, the San Francisco community or any other locale. But the word is not limited to a geographical reference, for we also speak of "the elderly community," the "legal community," the "nursing community," the "online community," and so forth. So it makes sense to think of a profession also as a sort of community, indeed a highly specialized one.

A profession is, by definition, an occupation which requires considerable education and specialized training. This combination of education and training equips one with a particular kind of power over others. In the legal profession, the power consists of both of knowledge of the law and of how the system of law operates. In healthcare, it consists of knowledge of various diagnoses, treatment options, and the economic implications for a patient and patient's family. Likewise in other professions, the specialized knowledge and training put the professional in a position of power over others, those who seek their assistance. At this point, Merton's perspective seems to imply that persons, in our case professionals specifically, find unity and wholeness not in an inner peace which might even take pride in personal success, but in recognition of a deep unity with others that is motivated by a conception of love that works itself out in both belief and practice.

By these lights then, the resolution of tensions in professional ethics (in particular, the navigation of so many of the so-called "gray areas") is not to be found by focusing on the "unity of the self" put forward by many so-called "self-help gurus" or in popular books which attempt to persuade people otherwise. Merton seems to deride the sort of holism that focuses on an inner peace which is actually grounded on a distinction which privileges one's self over others. This is not the proper way. On the contrary, for Merton the real path to unity of the self is through identification with others, a unity of the self with others which is manifest in his epiphany at the corner of a downtown city street. The task is to explore the implications of that epiphany for professional ethics.

Chapter Three

Contemporary Challenges in Professional Ethics

We have explored ways in which ethical theories and value systems have informed our attitudes and decisions toward work and our professional lives. Traditional theories of morality can enlighten us about the influences which help to formulate our everyday decisions. We also observed that ethical theories do not, of themselves, take positions on moral issues; rather, people use theoretical justifications to provide reasons for their choices. Theories cannot make the decision for you. Ethical theories alone cannot clarify the difficulties of moral dilemmas, especially the problems of professional life. So, moral theories are relevant to daily life; they expose fundamental principles for moral behavior and they provide a language through which we can offer justifications and reasons for our actions. But theories are limited in their application to real-world situations.

We also examined references to ethical perspectives in Merton's *Conjectures of a Guilty Bystander*, in particular his criticisms against some popular views. Some philosophers and social critics have argued that the diversity of moral perspectives and the contradictory conclusions which they draw are primarily due to the fragmentation of the modern self. Contrary to other views, Merton finds a resolution to the problem of the unity of the self in a profound recognition of a unity of the self with others Merton's call to the contemplative life, to meditation on this unity with others, needs to be explored in relation to professional ethics.

Therefore, it is important to sketch some of the major ethical issues in the professions. Several perennial questions in professional ethics come to mind: "Why do otherwise good people do bad things?" Moreover, since organizations have layers of management and decision-makers, "Who is responsible?" To the first question, one response has been to recognize that there can be a great tension between one's personal morality and role morality (that is, the moral values, perhaps articulated in a professional code of ethics, for any person occupying a particular role). How does one decide "the right thing to do" when one's professional responsibilities conflict with one's own moral sensitivities? This conundrum has given rise to much philosophical discussion for several decades, but I argue that Merton's reflections from *Conjectures of a Guilty Bystander* can also contribute a constructive response to this issue. To the second question, most responses focus on an individual agent acting in a given situation. When a moral failure comes to light in business, for example, the tendency (particularly from the view of the corporation involved) is to isolate the event to a single person or small group. However, exploring the relationship between individuals and institutions (especially as members of professions) casts this issue in a different light, just as Merton's concept of a "guilty bystander" challenges simplistic accounts of moral responsibility. Moreover, his notion of "Christian Socratism," critical self-reflection in light of spiritual values, means that we must confront the guilty bystander in ourselves; we must reject innocent bystanding, in our personal and professional lives.

Personal Morality and Role Morality

The fragmentation of the self into demarcated roles, each with its own priorities and responsibilities, influences and may obstruct the ability of an individual to act morally on deeply held values. Acting "professionally," especially on the basis of adherence to a specific code of ethics, can often lead to conflicts with one's own personal values and commitments. Moreover, in today's marketplace professionals are often at the intersection of roles and disciplines, so that even codes of ethics can conflict and become of little use.

The nature of the self is a topic that has a long history in Western philosophy. MacIntyre's account is heavily influenced by a traditional view that is traceable to seventeenth-century thinker Rene Descartes and the emergence of modern philosophy. MacIntyre is one of many contemporary philosophers and writers who focus on the nature of the self. Jean-Paul Sartre gives another description, albeit one that MacIntyre heavily criticizes. Although their two accounts differ dramatically in conceptual style and conclusion, I want to explore one similarity between their approaches. MacIntyre links authenticity with an Aristotelian conception of virtue, and associates morality with basic human nature. As we have seen, MacIntyre struggles to describe a holistic sense of self, which he believes is lost to history. Sartre argues against the notion that there is anything approaching "basic human nature." He attempts to express a conception of an authentic self, which he believes is distorted by conditions of "bad faith;" in fact, he has far more to say about the latter than the former.[1] Sartre finds it much easier to describe conditions of bad faith; he presupposes the value of authenticity. He believes that people live in the mode of bad faith most of the time throughout their lives. Arguably, however, some things that MacIntyre describes as fragmentation of the self resonate with things that Sartre expresses as "bad faith."

Sartre believes that human beings have radical freedom, the liberty to construct ourselves individually and to define collectively what it means to be human, apart from any divine being or God who might determine human nature. For Sartre, this radical freedom reveals our anguish: since we are the positors of meanings and values yet without any ultimate ontological or metaphysical grounds for justification, we find ourselves in anguish, weighed down by angst over our moral choices and their lack of resolution. For Sartre, angst is not a property of our consciousness, we *are* anguish. Fleeing from this anguish is, according to Sartre, bad faith. So irony, sarcasm, cynicism, lying are not examples of bad faith; these are directed outward toward others and do not necessarily affect the inner structure of consciousness. But those lies which are perpetrated from an ontological duality, which cut the psyche in two, as did Freud, these are indicative of bad faith—a negation of our freedom and responsibilities as individuals.

MacIntyre gives some good examples of the fragmentation of modernity. He describes a gentleman working in his garden and asks us to choose from a variety of descriptions—he is digging, taking exercise, gardening, preparing for winter, pleasing his wife, etc., and each description is equally correct but from different perspectives. For MacIntyre, the most accurate description is one that takes both social context and the intentions of the actor into account. "We cannot characterize behavior independently of intentions," argues MacIntyre, "and we cannot characterize intentions independently of the settings which make those intentions intelligible both to agents themselves and to others."[2] Any attempt to characterize behavior independent of context and intention runs the risk of equivocating on virtue. However, a single action may often involve a diversity of intentions, such that it can be difficult for even the actor to identify a "primary" intention as a motivation. Hence, the consequence of the fragmentation of the self, brought on by modernity, is the loss of a sense of virtue and goodness. As we have seen, MacIntyre argues:

> What are spoken of as the virtues of a good committee man or of a good administrator or of a gambler or a pool hustler are professional skills

professionally deployed in those situations where they can be effective, not virtues.[3]

Of course, social context and intentions imply relationships between actors and others, so interrelationships are a major factor in MacIntyre's account. He takes great issue with the individualism presupposed and defended in Sartre's account.

Sartre uses examples of a young coquette and a waiter. Imagine a woman going out with a particular man for the very first time. They are having a good time, the dinner and conversation have been excellent, and as they engage in conversation while waiting on dessert the man makes a simple gesture: he places his hand on hers. Now, says Sartre, the woman faces a choice—it may be a difficult decision but it is one that will most certainly determine how the rest of the evening (perhaps the rest of their lives) will go: she may choose to withdraw her hand, perhaps even with the rapidity that communicates, "Don't touch me." That would undoubtedly shape the rest of the evening . . ."Check please!" She might choose to return the man's caress, which would also send a meaningful message of its own. But Sartre asks us to imagine that she does not want to acknowledge her freedom, the necessity of her choice, so she turns the conversation to some lofty topic and leaves her motionless hand there on the table like a cold, dead fish. This woman, Sartre claims, is in bad faith.[4]

Consider a waiter in a restaurant. Sartre describes his motions as quick and a little too precise. He approaches the customers a little too rapidly; his demeanor and his voice express too much interest for the orders of the patrons. He even carries his tray with a feigned recklessness. He is playing a game, Sartre observes, he is playing at being a waiter. "The waiter in the café plays with his condition," says Sartre, "in order to realize it." Sartre then adds this poignant claim to his description, "this obligation is not different from that which is imposed on all tradesmen."[5] The waiter is in bad faith. While he knows that his existence, his being, transcends the role which he has at that moment, he is also aware that his performance is merely that—a performance, a *persona* for others and not his true self. His actions are merely a representation for others.

Likewise, using myself as an example: I am in bad faith whenever I approach my students "playing the game" of being a professor. Any time that I disguise a lack of concern for their academic performance with platitudes designed to comfort and dismiss them, I act in bad faith. My status as a professional provides me with certain duties, including moral responsibilities. As desirable as authenticity is, it is also difficult and downright impossible to maintain on a consistent basis. So, in the context of my institutional obligations, personal goals, and private problems, I sometimes play the game of being professor, just as surely as many of the members of my classes often play the game of being a student. There are times when I may be either unable or unwilling to meet the needs of a student, so I hide behind my professional status and its tangential responsibilities. Though I aspire to be an excellent teacher and to always be there for my students, I am unable to approximate that ideal. This is where Sartre leaves us, and the implications for professional life and management are worth further exploration.

Setting aside the question of who is right or wrong, or whose description is the most accurate for persons living in the twenty-first century, it is possible to see that both Sartre and MacIntyre contribute important insights to our self-understanding. Sartre's description of bad faith is a powerful one in which our anguish is revealed as freedom, it arises in spontaneity and recognition of our radical freedom as individuals. Why don't we, then, experience anguish straightforward more often? Because we hide behind common actions, meanings, and certain self-sustained values; we let things pass without reflection and we take cover behind appearances of order, structure, and conventional values.

I believe that Merton's perspective directs us toward a middle ground between these two positions. MacIntyre is correct to argue that modernity fragments the self like Humpty Dumpty falling off the wall, but he struggles to articulate the recovery of a holistic self rooted more in reality than in nostalgia; whereas Sartre concentrates almost exclusively on the individual and subjectivity, focusing more on those who direct their consciousness inward in a negative way. Merton's writing in *Conjectures* shares much in common with both existentialism and more traditional philosophy: he seems to agree with Sartre's view that we enter into bad faith by playing at the various roles which we occupy at any given time, but he disagrees that we are "condemned to be free" to a state of despair by our anxiety at the lack of any objective certainty in our lives. Merton describes throughout *Conjectures* the existential forces that influence both individuals and society. The "chaotic forces inside everybody" are neither chosen by us nor free for us to avoid. These chaotic forces are exacerbated by the variety of roles which we occupy at any given point in our lives: I am someone's son, someone's father, a husband; a citizen of this city, county, state and country, yet aspiring to be a "citizen of the world" and a critic of aspects of all these relationships; an employee, a professor and member of a profession, simultaneously a member of several other organizations; a parishioner yet a critic of religious institutions; the list could go on. I suspect the list might be similar for many others.

Merton points in a unique direction beyond MacIntyre and Sartre by emphasizing the unity of the self with others, as we have seen, and by putting action to that belief through acts of reconciliation. Several times in the *Conjectures of a Guilty Bystander* Merton speaks of reconciling differences in himself. He expresses amazement that people turn to his writings for "ready-to-serve" Catholic answers on all sorts of topics, and complains that, if people really *read* him, they would realize that he does not claim to have answers but (similar to Socrates) only some of the most pressing questions. Merton recounts the Christian existentialist Gabriel Marcel's claim that an artist who works to create effects for which he will be well-known is in bad faith. Merton asserts that, like the artist, we all fall prey to believing the self we've created out of inauthentic efforts to be our "real self" and our true identity. However, Merton claims, our real selves are hidden in mystery. For his part, Merton believed that his "job" was to clarify the tradition of which he was part, and which lived through him, and to reconcile ideological differences into himself by showing a path beyond those fragmentations and false appearances which separate people from one another.[6] Merton's grasp of his vocation has implications for our understanding of professional life and its ability to distort our selves.

Fragmentation of the self into a variety of roles, as portrayed by philosophers such as MacIntyre and Sartre, obstructs the ability to decide difficult moral choices at work by placing into conflict one's professional duties with one's personal values. The very concept of being a consummate professional in a given field is taken to mean the ability to make moral decisions consistent with that role. However, these duties and justifications on which they rely are often contrary to personal intuitions and values that people hold both more deeply and prior to becoming professionals.

Professional Roles and Ethical Dilemmas

Examples of these tensions and contrary intuitions abound in every profession, and are the hallmark of the chasm between professional ethics and personal morality. When confronted by ethical dilemmas, at best, we seek the wise counsel of a fellow professional or a close friend in whom to confide; at worst, we do not even realize that contradiction between our values and beliefs, condemning us to bad faith and a logic of failure. No profession, hence no professional, is immune from these conflicts.

Stanford University professor of law William Simon has written about the ethical conflicts which arise in the legal profession. For example, he tells the story of an early twentieth-century lawyer who receives information from his client that establishes the innocence of another person convicted of murder.[7] Because his client would not consent to the disclosure of that information, the lawyer remained silent as the innocent man remained and ultimately died in prison. Personal moral values and professional ethics come into obvious conflict in this situation. No reasonable person would condone the suffering of an innocent person wrongfully convicted. Nevertheless, the rules that govern the profession of lawyering, namely attorney-client privilege, forbid the un-consented disclosure of information received from a client. In this situation the lawyer's own commitment to justice is constrained by a rule of his profession (the rule being based on justice also, with adequate theoretical justifications which support it) so that by following the rule the lawyer participates in an unethical situation with an unjust result.

Of course, this is just one example, and a bit of an extreme one, of a myriad of ethical conflicts faced by attorneys on a daily basis.[8] Simon asks us to consider a scenario in which government has provided some subsidy in support of small family farms, defined in the statute as one hundred sixty acres or less.[9] Suppose then that larger, wealthier landowners approach their attorneys also seeking to benefit from the subsidy, which the lawyers could do through legal means by creatively gaming the system in order for their clients to qualify for the government support. Forming a company, the clients disburse small tracts of land to family members, each of whose "farm" qualifies for and receives the subsidy while the client retains ownership and control of the farm as a whole. Though it might be easy to wax eloquent about a poorly written statute that allowed such circumvention, or to distinguish glibly between the letter and spirit of the law, both of these responses ignore or trivialize the pressures faced by the lawyer. Suppose you are the attorney and your long-standing client, who also happens to be your neighbor and friend of the family, comes to you with this proposal and an expectation that you will make it possible for them to receive a large cash subsidy. What would you do?

Such dilemmas arise in the health care profession too. Krzysztof Kieslowski, in his magnificent set of short films entitled *The Decalogue*, tells the story of a physician placed in a bind between personal beliefs and professional duties.[10] For a lengthy time the doctor has been treating Andrej for a serious and possibly terminal disease, which has left Andrej barely conscious and unable to communicate. The doctor is approached by Andrej's wife, Dorota, who insists on knowing from the doctor whether Andrej will live or die. Several times the doctor resists her request, citing the little-known nature of the disease and of the poorly understood nature of its treatment, and refusing to pass judgment on Andrej's chances for recovery or to condemn him to an early death. In a final act of desperation, Dorota confronts the physician and explains her situation: she is happily married to Andrej, he has always been supportive and loving, but there was one thing that he could not give her—a baby. Now she is pregnant by another man, whom she also claims to love, but the timetable during which she can obtain a legal abortion is almost exhausted. She pressures the doctor, demanding to know the fate of her husband: if he is to die, she wants to have the child and build a relationship with the father; but if he is going to live, she wants to preserve her good marriage by having an abortion. Although the doctor attempts to evade her placement of him into this dilemma, she schedules an abortion for the next day and confronts him one last time, at the very least to insist that his conscience cannot be clear. Whenever I have used this episode in a course, I ask students, "If you were the doctor, what would you do?" Hiding behind HIPAA-type rules, patient privacy regulations, or professional codes will not help much with this decision.

    This scenario is intense and perhaps far-fetched, but it is symbolic of the difficult ethical dilemmas faced by healthcare professionals on a daily basis. Nurses are often confronted with ethical dilemmas, caught between the needs of the patient, the demands of physician, and the rules and policies of the institutions for which they work. Some of the moral conflicts that they face may seem simple and relatively easy to resolve, but the far-reaching consequences of their actions and the import of their decisions for the lives of others make even the most casual circumstances into potentially significant events. Suppose a woman visits her physician for treatment of a chronic illness, and the physician persuades the patient to begin a controversial form of therapy. After talking to the physician, the woman stops by the nurse's station to pick up a prescription to begin the therapy. In the course of conversation, the nurse realizes that the physician has not informed the patient that other treatment options are available. What should the nurse do?

    These dilemmas take their toll on professionals, inflicting emotional and spiritual harm, and damaging persons' lives. Unless a person detaches her or his personal life from his or her professional role, a further fragmentation of the self, the person is exposed to what Jeff Schmidt has characterized as "soul battering." In his book, *Disciplined Minds*, Schmidt recounts the findings of New York psychologist Herbert Freudenberger, who coined the term "burnout" decades ago: the personal consequences of alienation at work include, "cynicism, disconnection, loss of vitality and authenticity, decreased enjoyment of family life, anger, strained relationship with spouse or partner, divorce, obsessive behavior, chronic fatigue, poor eating habits, neglect of friends, social isolation, loneliness—and the list of symptoms goes on."[11] The psychological and spiritual pain of moral conflicts is difficult to measure, but it can cause persons to abandon their profession for another career or to remain—however bitterly and alienated—in a job that they despise. In his book *My Job, My Self*, Al Gini tells the story of an emergency room physician whom he met while working as an orderly in a hospital. Gini observed this physician in many trauma situations, always with a coolheaded demeanor and an excellent bedside manner, fighting to save lives while showing care and comforting people, sometimes in their final moments of life. On one occasion when Gini expressed his admiration to the physician, he was immediately rebuffed. "That is all just the result of good training," he said. What he did not like was dealing with patients; hence, his choice of emergency room duty. He only had to deal with the immediate problem at hand, and then he could pass the patient on to someone else. Speaking bluntly, he did not like people. The physician explained to Gini, "I simply learned to make a game out of it."[12] How reminiscent of Sartre's waiter!

The same types of moral conflicts also confront educators. Imagine a teacher attempting to help a young child with some learning difficulties. The teacher is certain that the child could benefit from additional resources and specialized instruction; moreover, the extra time and attention given to this young child detracts from the regular flow and progress for the other students in the class. However, the school system has a policy which mandates that only students who score below a particular threshold on a scrupulous test shall qualify for the additional resources. The child's score on the exam is barely above the mark, making the child ineligible for assistance. How should the teacher respond?

The difficulties of navigating through these sorts of moral conflicts are heightened in the context of the twenty-first century global workplace. It is becoming increasingly common to recognize jobs which are at the intersection of two or more professions. Linda Peeno has called these multidisciplinary occupations, "hybrid professions." Her own experience as a physician working for a health insurance company is a primary example of a hybrid professional.[13] The conflict of interest dilemmas alone would overwhelm a person, as the individual attempts to make moral decisions while occupying multiple professional roles at once. How should Peeno respond to a request for an extensive surgery? As a physician bound by the Hippocratic Oath with duties to the health of persons, or bound as an agent of the company with duties to management and shareholders? The hybrid professional is an employee who operates at the conjunction of two or more fields, and is thus confronted with situations beyond those that merely bring into conflict ethical norms of a particular role and our most commonly held values. New books with titles like *Biomedical Ethics for Engineers* bear witness to this phenomenon and growing trend in business.[14] The hybrid professional can have more than one applicable standard of judgment of ethical issues that is supposed to govern their field. Because these multi-disciplinary positions are on the edge of the frontier, there is a lack of precedent and of consistent moral reflection to guide one. A physician or nurse working with the marketing division of a managed care organization (HMO) faces, in some ways, unique ethical conflicts that do not seem to be captured by traditional ethical theories or professional codes of ethics. To the physician- or nurse-executive, having more than one code of ethics is for practical purposes as good as having none. In a given ethical dilemma, which set of theoretical principles, professional values, or code of ethics ought to be followed? These health care business professionals sometimes make the observation that since they do not have direct patient contact, many of the traditional values in bioethics do not apply to their work. As a result, many would argue that they not only do not *have to* "think like a doctor," they *should not* think like doctors. In keeping with this view, their health management or MBA programs and academic business ethics courses typically do not focus on specific ethical issues that are unique to the managed care context in which they work. Hence, whatever education they may have received in bioethics does not easily apply to the business of managed care, and whatever education they received in business ethics does not cover the complex issues of medical ethics.

Ethical Conflicts and Moral Distress

Cognitive dissonance is a term that psychologists use to describe the discomfort, tension, and stress one feels when trying to hold on to conflicting beliefs, but it also aptly expresses one's feelings when personal values and professional responsibilities are contradictory. In such circumstances, codes of ethics or company mission statements seem to be of little help in resolving an ethical dilemma. In addition to dilemmas, however, there are situations of moral distress: instances in which one has a sense of the "right thing to do" but is obstructed from that course of action by regulation, conflicting obligations, professional, even personal pressures. One might respond to a situation, similar to the scenarios already mentioned, by compartmentalizing one's self-identity: "my personal moral beliefs are just that, personal; because this is a work related issue I should act consistently with my professional responsibilities." But such a response only deepens the fragmentation of the self, described by MacIntyre. Alternatively, one might attempt to ignore the issue, to let the situation play itself out. Like the physician in Kieslowski's drama, one might attempt to hide behind professional standards and evasive reactions. This option however leads squarely into bad faith, which, as Sartre describes, commits one to an inauthentic existence.

Neither of these alternatives is satisfactory. Each one, in its own way, places a person in the mode of "guilty bystanding," which Merton persuasively argues against. He is clearly influenced by existentialist philosophy in his assertion that we construct a pseudo-self, which exists only as appearance for others and which masks our more true or genuine self. This constructed self, which exists solely as an appearance for others, is the source of anguish and anxiety because it lacks authenticity and hope. Merton instead argues for critical self-reflection, an internal dialectic of openness, critique, and renewal. Recalling the figure of Socrates, he believes that contemplation on one's way of being in the world is a means of self-discovery and clarification. Speaking of Pope John XXIII in this regard, Merton states, "fidelity to the Socratic principle is essential to our Western cultural tradition."[15] The exercise of dialectic in contemplation deepens and advances our natural-given desire for truth and it clarifies our understanding by centering our lives between the twin faults of passive indifference or disconnected series of knee-jerk reactions. This contemplative act of self-examination gives one access to a "most hidden self, the self we do not experience every day, and perhaps never experience, though it is always there."[16] In the light of self-discovery and clarification of purpose, there emerges hope, not only for the future but also for the present. It is the creative power of this present hope that allows one to accept one's place in the world and one's tasks, and to do so, as Merton says, "liberated from the limitations of the world and of a restricted halfhearted milieu."[17] Why "restricted"? Because we are constrained by institutions, professions, codes, and organizational hierarchies, which pressure us into conformity with their proposed ends and values. Why is it "halfhearted"? Because under the pressures of these systems people often capitulate to contextual pressures, surrendering their progress toward truth, abandoning hope, and conflating appearance for authenticity. Merton's insightfulness is confirmed by the experience of Al Gini with his physician colleague, and as Jeff Schmidt shows, it is reinforced in corporations, firms, businesses, and organizations on a daily basis. It is even applicable to educational institutions in which professors no longer aspire to be excellent teachers and mentors, but regard themselves as freelance scholars, automatically deserving any benefits or personal advantages afforded by academic systems, which were nevertheless designed and intended for the benefit of students.

Hence, critical self-reflection is a path to freedom, a liberation from institutional obfuscations and professional systems. Contemplative dialectic is a means by which we may, "completely and honestly accept ourselves, our own problems, our own defeat, with the creative consent and responsibility that unite us to God's will."[18] It is not about finding my place in the world, that approach ultimately is all about me; rather, it is about finding the world's place in me. In his book, *Forgetting Ourselves On Purpose*, Brian Mahan suggests that although our culture encourages ambition and celebrates the ferocity used to pursue it, we are often clueless about what we really want.[19] We are reluctant to admit, however, that our ambitions and desires are often prepackaged for us, including an owner's manual with directions on how to tailor them to suit your individual tastes. Nevertheless, critical self-reflection takes one in a different direction. In the spirit of Socrates dictum, "Know thyself!" contemplative dialectic directs one toward a spiritual freedom, which results from recognizing one's ambitions and desires, their sources, and seeing them for what they are. This liberation provides a person with the insight and power to avoid sacrificing oneself for things that only enslave.

Merton points out that so much of society lacks this freedom precisely because of a willingness to compromise one's self by purchasing lower freedoms at the price of higher ones. To do so is to auction off one's personal integrity, one's authentic self, for the sake of financial success, security, or just to be left alone (albeit in bad faith). The introspection which Merton encourages us to undertake, the self-questioning of one's deepest held spiritual and moral values, is the means to give one's life a sense of wholeness. It provides the foundation for the unity of oneself with others, placing one in harmony with the universal human spirit.

Individuals and Institutions

As employees, we become members of businesses, firms, corporations, and institutions in which we routinely go about our administrative tasks, seldom recognizing the indirect ways (sometimes direct) that we participate in unethical practices and systems. Our participation, in the forms of words, deeds, or even acts of omission, creates a ripple effect, which rolls out as tiny injustices (sometimes into larger ones) that proceed far beyond our cubicle or office.

In his book, *Trust*, noted historian Francis Fukuyama argues that Western civilization and contemporary culture is based on a presupposition of trust, even between strangers.[20] This disposition toward trust permeates our society and shapes our personal lives. It is such a natural component of our cultural atmosphere that, like the air we breathe, it is invisible or transparent to us. We eagerly and unreflectively enter into trusting relationships on a daily basis with persons whom we do not know: I trust the waiter who brings the food to my table, that it is wholesome and untainted. However, I have no idea, outside of unusual circumstances, who this person is! I know nothing of his background, family life, socioeconomic status, beliefs, or values. When I go to the supermarket, I trust that the grocer, whom I do not know, is placing healthy food and safe products on the shelves; I am even trusting persons unseen and perhaps far away, who placed the vegetables in the cans, that they contain the right ingredients and that they are safe and good. Likewise, when I purchase something from a vending machine, I implicitly trust the persons who process those products, the people who package and transport them, and the people who place them in the machine, that these drinks and snacks are genuine.

When beginning a new job with a company, many of which pay their employees on a monthly basis, I trust that my new employer is going to pay me—enough trust that I am willing to work an entire month without remuneration, hoping but by no means assured that at the end of that month I will receive my pay. Whenever we purchase a vehicle, put fuel in our cars, enroll in a class at university, rush into hospital with an emergency, seek legal advice, and a host of other actions, we are implicitly though sometimes skeptically placing trust in the individuals who offer these products and services to us. If I happen to know the individual grocer or salesperson, the relationship is clearer and seems simple enough. The attribution of moral responsibility seems relatively straightforward when we are interacting with persons on an individual basis. However, we also enter into relationships with corporations and institutions, the relationship is much more complex and often murky, and the application of moral responsibility becomes ambiguous and often dubious. Even though our interactions are with individuals who occupy various roles with the institution, ultimately and somewhat awkwardly our relationship is held to be primarily with the organization. Therefore, we expand our trust not only to these individuals but also to a collective of which they are a part and which they represent in their particular roles.

This element of trust must function not only externally between the institution and those outside of it, but internally among the individuals who collectively constitute the organization. For the most part, we trust our colleagues and coworkers, and likewise they trust us, that we are fulfilling our roles and responsibilities. On a daily basis, failures and letdowns notwithstanding, as associates we trust one another to perform our assigned tasks and to do so in morally responsible ways.

That presumption of trust, with its corresponding sense of group loyalty, is so strongly held that it becomes difficult to make morally responsible choices whenever doing so might be seen as contrary to the group or institution. For example, whistle blowing is not an option that people undertake lightly. In fact, "whistle blowing" is about as neutral a term as we have for that activity. Other words and phrases that we use include snitch, rat, "narc" (when I was growing up this meant drugs were involved, but today's youth apply it to any case), tattletale, fink, and others. What do all of these words have in common? They are all negative. We really have no positive word for this action, "whistle blowing" is the most indifferent concept we have for it. Our language betrays our bad faith and moral reasoning; for even if one feels a duty to speak out in a given situation, even if one believes that to do so would bring about the greatest good for the greatest number, and especially in circumstances where to do so will benefit the individual personally, the unspoken message from our culture and our organizations is: "you had better keep your mouth shut!"

In my graduate bioethics and MBA courses, I typically introduce the moral decision-making process with a relatively simple and straightforward case. "Suppose you become aware that a fellow classmate is engaging in academic dishonesty. You have evidence that you could present, should it be necessary, so there is no ambiguity. This person is cheating. What would you do?" I have been keeping an informal poll over the years, as we discuss this scenario. To this day, I could still count on one hand the number of students who say that they would report the cheater. Some students claim that they would confront the cheater personally, in private. Phil McGraw, "Dr. Phil" to many television viewers, has a catchy phrase that sounds very Socratic to me, in a laid-back way, which I like to use in these types of exchanges: "How's that working out for you?" So I engage those graduate students who claim that, rather than reporting, they would confront the person. "How's that discussion going to go?" I ask them to role-play that conversation with me. Most students determine, that's not working out so well. The majority admit that ultimately, they would blow off the situation, just let it go, choosing not to get involved. Even if the professor is grading on a curve, which means that the grades of everyone else in the class might be diminished, most students still choose to look the other way. Thus, I continue our discussion and role-playing by assigning one student the role of professor in the course. "Professor, you have a cheater in your class. Do you want to know?" The vast majority of students will answer yes, justifying their response by appealing to values such as, the fairness of the grading process, and the integrity of their own course—their personal integrity as a professional in academia. What a difference from a few moments ago! As a fellow student, the person chose to take no action or, at best, to say something offhanded to the cheater, but now the person is extolling the importance of fairness and integrity. Occasionally I will get a few students who claim that even as a professor, if the members of this class were not willing to come forward with the information, then they still have no desire to know. So, I will assign another student with the role of Dean of the institution, "You have a professor in your school who would rather not know about academic dishonesty in the class. How's that working out for you?" Almost invariably, as Deans, students will oppose the professor's point of view, citing the value of the degrees that are awarded, the honor and reputation of the institution. At this point in our discussion, it then becomes obvious to students how our values shift so easily depending on one's role. Still, abandoning the role-playing exercise and returning to their actual role as students, they will continue to express their reluctance to take any action in this situation. I then surprise them with the knowledge that their own graduate program has an honor code clause, which they all agreed to as a condition of entrance to the program, which obligates them to report instances of academic dishonesty. Ratting, snitching, blowing the whistle on someone is simply not something that they would want to do, even after explicitly agreeing to a duty to do so.

This is a short and simple case, though not without its complex features. Often students will ask about whether or not they are friends with the hypothetical cheater. That can definitely change the tone, even the possibility, of the proposed private conversation. If they are not friends but competing for the top position in their cohort, their decision seems to be much easier. The contextual features serve to give this case its complexity, but real life is this way too. Whenever we are confronted by those daily, innocuous looking, simple choices, we do so in the context of other roles and responsibilities that we have. Our context is deeper than one's situation. We are limited and shaped by our historical, socioeconomic, political, and religious backgrounds. Perhaps our attraction to a particular moral theory or perspective is also rooted in these influences. Likewise, our participation in a variety of institutions and organizations shapes our moral outlook. Institutions help to define one's self-identity.

Institutions also have moral dispositions. As we organize ourselves collectively, especially in businesses and professions, those organizations develop cultures of their own, including beliefs and values. Reminiscent of

Plato's view that "society is the individual writ large," institutions take on characteristics of the individuals that comprise them. Organizations are "individuals writ large." As though in reference to an individual, we might even say that institutions may have their own personality and character. However, the relationship works both ways: by participating in these institutions we begin to take on some of these personality traits as individuals; we may even begin to act on the basis of the character of an organization of which we are a part. To the extent that we do, we allow the organization to define our personhood. Worst case scenario, we do this unreflectively and lose ourselves in our work, allowing the institution to determine right and wrong for us.

The same can be generally said for a profession. Our education and training serve to indoctrinate us into specialized ways of seeing and interacting with the world and with people. Professional commitments have the power to shape our own outlook on life. Eric Mount tells the story of a student who protested against having to take a required theology class: "That's messing with my life!" was the gist of the student's protest. Mount pointed out to the student that the entire educational process amounts to messing with one's life![21] Any genuine liberal arts education, if it is worth its salt, ought to modify one's core beliefs and values. It is "liberal" not in the sense that it is left of mainstream values, that is a misnomer. Such an education is *liberal* in the sense that it's ultimate goal is *freedom*; the knowledge and skills developed by a graduate in such an environment are intentionally crafted to liberate the student, providing that person with the information and dexterity to be successful in any environment, regardless of the temporary circumstances. The focus, unlike a technical or trade school, is on learning how to learn, to teach one's self, learning that is self-directed and self-managed. The high division of labor and changing nature of work in Western society is dependent on workers with these abilities. A liberal arts education, in its ideal form, ought to give its bearer the opportunity and the wherewithal to pursue any profession at any point in one's life.

For Merton this includes education that broadens one's perspective by encouraging the exploration of other perspectives and traditions. However, a genuine liberal arts education, in the spirit of Thomas Merton, encounters two immediate obstacles. The first is, to borrow a phrase from Allan Bloom, a closing of the mind by a rejection of otherness, of that which is foreign or different, with a prejudiced preference for that which is familiar and safe. The second impediment is the tendency to play the game of acceptance and tolerance, without genuinely encountering or listening to others whose views differ from one's own. For Merton the wholeness of life is not to be found in a retreat to the pseudo-security of an isolated individualism, but the deepest unity of the self is to be found in a broadening of the self through acceptance and grace—that is, a profound love and appreciation for otherness and an acceptance of difference as it is.

This is precisely the point where Merton's call to contemplation becomes relevant for us. Merton attacks, as he puts it, "the sham, the unreality, the alienation, the forced systematization of life."[22] By participating in organizations and professions, we allow our self-understanding to be manipulated by the social structures of which we are a part. Like the waiter in Sartre's example, our language and our gestures become exaggerated. We have come to accept the role of playing the professional, compromising our integrity by resigning ourselves to conditions of bad faith.

This concept of a forced systematization of life may sometimes be an accurate description of professional life. As noted above, it often begins with one's professional education and training, and becomes more acute with the advancement of one's career. Merton likens going to work for a business (we could add profession) to joining a religion. Similarly, Jeff Schmidt argues in *Disciplined Minds* that a profession should not be defined as a skill but as an ideology, a system of ideas and values which justify particular actions. Ideology provides the context in which we determine whether actions are right or wrong, justified or unjustified, including not only our evaluations of others but also ourselves. In this sense, ideology has long been a part of the workplace. Employers screen applicants to verify their qualifications and skills, however, they also examine and assess the attitudes and personality traits of potential employees. Schmidt suggests that even technical exams like the GRE and LSAT are more than tools for the measurement of professional qualifications, these neutral looking tests gauge ways of thinking and character traits. Beyond demonstrating one's proficiency in a specialized area of knowledge, these and other professional exams provide some indication as to the extent to which a person can follow the ideological lead of a profession, its institutions, and future employers.[23]

Following the ideological lead becomes increasingly important to a global marketplace in which the nature of work is dramatically shifting. Under the pressure of opportunities for advancements or merely holding on to one's job, employees submit to the demands of playing sham games of acceptance and tolerance, without genuinely encountering or listening to others, whose views differ from their own. Work becomes the structuring principle, the central pillar of organization around which we build our lives: the way in which we spend our time, the persons with whom we associate, even our choice of leisure activities. Work structures our daily schedules and routines. What we do during our waking hours for most of our adult lives is centered around when and where we work. Just the trip to it, "the commute," can daily consume more than two hours for many people. Our place of work also determines to some extent who our friends are. Whether we think of them as associates, colleagues, acquaintances, or friends, these are the people that we spend a majority of our time with. It is no wonder that people often find their life-partners (or choose to be unfaithful to one) at their places of employment; it is where they spend most of their time. Moreover, even our life away from work is shaped by our employment. The kinds of things that we come to desire, the vacation spots we prefer to visit, the other things that we do when we are away from work can be influenced by our choice of work. This tendency of work to structure our lives, to be the central organizing feature, is inherently linked to its capacity to provide our lives with meaning and purpose. It is what gives work its ideological power and creates the need, perhaps even the desire, for the forced systematization of life.

Corporate Selves and Values

In order for institutions and corporations to maximize their profitability, it simply has not been feasible to create higher layers and layers of management to monitor the productivity of workers. Rather, it has become necessary to educate and train workers to manage themselves, which means narrowing their perceived scope of freedom in order to develop uncritical, compliant producers who are loyal to the institutional ideology. By our participation in institutions, organizations, and professions, we gradually become anesthetized into guilty bystanders. Our embeddedness in professions and organizations, shaped by the ideological nature of our education, training, and institutional atmosphere, inclines us towards conformity, silence, and passive indifference. The ominous pressure from our professional peers is enough to ensure that we function within the ideological box, secure in our faith that by abiding by the rules and the approved code of ethics, our choices and actions are justified. So, we routinely go about our administrative tasks, seldom questioning or critically reflecting on the ethical implications of our ordinary activities. Dietrich Dörner describes this type of uncritical, unreflective routine-following behavior as "the logic of failure."[24] Dörner contends that we build failure *into* systems and organizations. Failure, he says has its own logic, its own structure. When we organize ourselves in particular ways and fail to plan for contingencies that will arise in the systematic process we have constructed, we are practicing the logic of failure. One can think of some famous examples such as the space shuttle *Challenger* disaster, Chernobyl, the Exxon *Valdez*, or the response to Hurricane Katrina, but Dörner maintains that we practice the logic of failure in small ways on an almost daily basis. When we fail to save money for a rainy day, we are practicing the logic of failure. When Enron employees had their 401(k) plans totally invested with Enron stock, they were exhibiting the logic of failure. Most recently, when regulators, bankers, investors, and consumers allowed the subprime mortgage market to expand beyond oversight and control, it was set up for the logic of failure.[25] We set ourselves up in the logic of failure whenever we uncritically and unreflectively go through our professional and personal lives.

It is not the case that institutions are inherently bad, certainly not evil. There are numerous examples of corporations "doing the right thing" in difficult circumstances. Johnson & Johnson's decision, in 1982, to pull all bottles of Tylenol from the shelves has become a classic example. Although tainted doses were ultimately found to be confined to the greater-Chicago area, decision-makers and leadership at the company decided to remove the entire product from stores across the United States. Of course, at the time of their decision, the leaders of Johnson & Johnson had no assurance that their action would guarantee that no more customers would be harmed, much less that the reputation of the product and the company would be preserved. Nevertheless, the harm to customers was contained and the social status of both the product and the corporation increased dramatically. In fact, the tamper resistant packaging found on most products today is a result of Johnson & Johnson's response to this crisis. Institutions are capable of doing the right thing in moments of crisis; contrary to the sentiments of some versions of egoism, there is nothing intrinsically wrong with belonging to a group or participating in a social network. Human beings are horde, not herd, animals. Organizing ourselves collectively seems to be a natural human activity. It is certainly a contributing factor to human flourishing.

Nevertheless, something happens to us as individuals whenever we become part of a larger group. Our own moral sensitivities become diminished and are superseded by the values of the group as a whole or of its leaders. Whenever we perceive ourselves to be part of a larger group, for example, as members of a profession, the tendency is toward passive indifference or subordination to the demands of those who are in charge. A classic example, mentioned earlier, became known as the Kitty Genovese case. In 1964, Ms. Genovese was attacked outside of her home in the early hours of the morning. Neighbors and passersby heard her screams, but no one came to her assistance. Frightened away, her attacker left the scene, though only to retrieve a large brim hat in hopes of not being recognized. On his return, the attack continued and ultimately he sexually assaulted her as she lay dying. The entire incident spanned one half hour. According to a later *New York Times* report, thirty-eight people witnessed the attack on Ms. Genovese, but no one made an attempt to save her life. Though passive indifference in a professional setting seldom involves the death of a person, there can be no doubt that it contributes to unethical practices and small injustices that harm those who are involved.

Another classic example, which involves an institutional context, is the famous Zimbardo experiment at Stanford University. In 1971, groups of students were recruited from volunteers to participate as guards and inmates in a mock prison. Students were assigned their roles based on personality types. The experiment was canceled after a few days because students adapted so rapidly to their roles. Guards became increasingly menacing and sadistic toward the prisoners. The lead researcher, Professor Zimbardo, halted the experiment after a graduate student complained about the level of inhumane treatment, and pointed out that he was passively allowing it. There seems little doubt that participation in institutional settings and holding positions of power, as professionals do, can modify one's moral outlook even to the point of engaging in unethical behavior. This is how education can contribute to this negative aspect, for it emphasizes respect for authority and reinforces doing as one is told. Professional training may also add to this, because it mandates "this is how we do things," even to the point at which morally questionable acts become a matter of routine.

As a monk, Thomas Merton was certainly no stranger to institutional hierarchy or organizational power. He was clearly familiar with the importance of recognizing authority and complying with assigned roles. However, in *Conjectures of a Guilty Bystander*, Merton speaks forcefully against "submission to organized injustice."[26] Concepts like resignation, servile acquiescence, and submission have no place in Merton's philosophical perspective. He constantly reinforces the value of freedom and eschews blaming others for one's own failures. Rather, Merton fuses the concept of freedom with personal responsibility, a freedom which is exercised from critical self-reflection and dialectic. Without these two forces of self-reflection and dialectic, Merton's notion of "Christian Socratism," we set ourselves up for the logic of failure: through education and training we become members of professions, going about our daily routines in monotonous fashion, and without thinking contribute to questionable deeds and systems of organization.

Moral Failure and the Corporate Self

Merton intensely focuses on one of the most egregious examples of moral failure, Adolf Eichmann, infamous high-ranking member of Hitler's Nazi regime and architect of their plan to eradicate the Jewish people. He fled to Argentina after World War II, where he lived under an alias until captured and taken to Israel to stand trial for "crimes against humanity." He was hanged after being found guilty. Hannah Arendt sat through the entire trial, writing for the *New York Times*, and later published a book, *Eichmann in Jerusalem*, about the trial and her observations. Arendt's book had a profound effect on Merton. In his writings, he connected the professionalism of Eichmann with his notion of guilty bystanding. Merton's analysis first appears as, "A Devout Meditation in Memory of Adolf Eichmann," in his book, *Raids on the Unspeakable*, which was published just prior to *Conjectures of a Guilty Bystander*. Merton begins that essay by expressing his astonishment that a psychiatric examination deemed Eichmann perfectly sane. His actions would be more understandable if he were diagnosed as psychotic. Merton penetrates the dark irony that a person considered calm and well-balanced could daily go about his administrative job at his desk in such a conscientious and orderly manner, completely undisturbed that his official duty was the organization of mass murder. He had no sense of guilt. On the contrary, Eichmann demonstrated a respect for law and order, he was obedient and loyal to the system. He seems to have been motivated by a deep sense of duty, even to the point of self-sacrifice: a first-hand tour of the facilities at Auschwitz may have disturbed him to the point of going weak in the knees but, as Merton describes Eichmann, he simply considered it "just the routine unpleasantness of the daily task." One must shoulder the burden of daily monotonous work for the good of the organization. Eichmann was reasonable; he was utilitarian. Eichmann was proud of his job. But Merton exposes the madness and bad faith of this sort of participation in a system or institution by condemning its apparent reasonableness and pseudo-justification. "The whole concept of sanity," claims Merton, "in a society where spiritual values have lost their meaning is itself meaningless."[27] Persons can appear reasonable and their actions justifiable when they act in an orderly and dependable way, consistent with expectations of the roles and institutions to which they belong. This is role morality at its worst. It is also the ultimate manifestation of guilty bystanding.

Merton's analysis of Eichmann continues in *Conjectures of a Guilty Bystander*. His insights may seem unsettling, particularly to a "feel-good" culture intent on denying the burden, if not the reality, of guilt. Merton's scrutiny of Eichmann's story is disturbing, in part, because we want to believe in our own goodness. We do not want to accept—much less bear the burden of—the possibility that in fulfilling our ordinary responsibilities we might actually be causing harm. Eichmann's primary justification, "I was simply following orders," though no longer a permissible *legal* defense, still covers up so many *routine daily tasks* and responses to organizational demands that one might otherwise find morally questionable and repugnant. Merton's discussion suggests that there is no justification for believing that "market failures" (which are really "people failures" at base) originate only from "bad" people. It should not be surprising that many market failures have moral failures as their catalyst. When a market crashes, a corporation fails, or a profession experiences the black eye from some misdeed, it is seldom the sole fault of one bad person acting in isolation. This is precisely the point of Dörner's concept of a "logic of failure." Merton's notion of guilty bystanding exposes the reality that we, as coworkers, colleagues, neighbors, and fellow citizens, help construct and contribute to ethical collapses. The moral failures that we help to construct, through a sort of premeditated carelessness, are pervasive and deep. The message of Merton's *Conjectures of a Guilty Bystander* is that moral disasters, certainly like Eichmann's but including the small ones which happen every day, stand as an indictment of all society.

Blind obedience and an unquestioning deontological-like sense of duty can only give the superficial appearance of goodness, not its actuality. That approach to life, especially professional life, leads to participation in organized injustice. The desire for structure and order in one's life, which is provided by membership in an institution or organization, cannot justify retreat from personal responsibility. Accountability seems more palatable when it is to an institution, because it relieves me of the personal existential necessity of taking responsibility for myself, for my actions, acting out of freedom instead of blind loyalty. But the attempt to shift responsibility in this way ultimately fails since it is an act of bad faith. Although one might mistakenly hope that reason and conscience have been made superfluous by institutional mission statements, the employee handbook, or codes of ethics, Merton reminds us that neither bureaucracy nor blind rule-following can ensure that one is pursuing goodness.

One response to these issues is to attempt to legislate social and institutional values through regulation. In the United States, agencies such as the Federal Trade Commission, the Securities and Exchange Commission, the Equal Employment Opportunity Commission, and the Occupational Safety and Health Administration are prime examples. Other forms of external constraints are also commonplace, including state licensure boards and additional regulatory agencies. However, this approach runs the risk of reducing the *moral* to the *legal* sphere. There are numerous examples which demonstrate that the right thing to do morally may not be consistent with what is legal. Martin Luther King Jr., in his famous "Letter from a Birmingham Jail" argues that there is a moral law which supersedes legal prohibitions, and further, that citizens have a fundamental moral duty to disobey unjust law.[28] According to King, this disobedience must not take the form of trying to circumvent the law, but acts of "civil disobedience" should be done openly and with acceptance of the legal penalty in order to demonstrate to society as a whole that the law is in fact unjust. Even if it were possible, it might not be desirable to regulate everything that might be found offensive to others and to make such actions subject to enforcement. There is little doubt that laws do not receive equal enforcement, depending on the enforcer (another example of issues for professional ethics in related disciplines).

Alternatively, internal constraints may be used in lieu of external ones. Institutions may employ the use of disciplinary codes, human resource consultants, institutional review boards, or the latest trend—corporate ethics officers (a different "CEO") both to develop and to enforce institutional policies. Organizations may sometimes find these helpful, as may employees. However, these internal organizational constraints are similar to external ones in that it becomes a matter of enforcement, and employees may ultimately dismiss these internal structures as mere public relations or worse, as somewhere between comical and irritating. Institutional culture can set the tone concerning ethical standards and internal constraints, but this typically comes from the top of the organization down to employees, not from the lower strata of workers upwards to management.

However, there would seem to be a vast gray area between the coerciveness of external forces and the constraints of the internal structures. Of the former, Merton warns against private resignation to a presumed duty to authority. Doing so demonstrates a lack of self-understanding and depth. Though he is explicitly speaking about attempts to institute Gandhian nonviolence, his words are equally applicable to various attempts to externally regulate institutions. External regulation becomes a favorable option because, in the words of Merton,

> our lives have become a moral debacle, and enslavement to half-truths, in which we are the passive prey of totalitarian forces. We are ruled, and resigned to let ourselves be led, by our own weakness and by the prejudices of those who, more guilty and more frustrated than ourselves, need to exercise great power.[29]

Not to be confused with populist political rhetoric, Merton should not be construed as supporting efforts of massive deregulation; rather, I take Merton to be making the point that the so-called "self-regulation" of markets, industries, corporations, and professions makes no sense unless that regulation "trickles down" from the highest bureaucratic levels to the individual worker. It makes no sense to talk about the self-regulation of a profession unless you and I, as members of that profession, develop the capacity and willingness to regulate ourselves.

On the other hand, internal codes and constraints do little to encourage good moral decision-making; to the contrary, these mechanisms are generally designed simply to discourage poor decisions. In *Conjectures of a Guilty Bystander*, Merton asserts that rather than people ruling by power, power rules through people.[30] It rules us through other people, because the power is not "theirs" as such. This power comes from the collective nature of the institution itself, which attempts to justify its ideology through mission statements and moral codes. The only requirement is adherence to the policies of the code. At the very least, surrendering to it through passive indifference merely contributes a sense of credibility to the justifications and rationalizations which masquerade as good intentions. At most, to actively and longingly advocate unquestioning allegiance to these internal constraints is to surrender the freedom which makes us most fully human. If the power that we possess as professionals "rules through us" in some sense, then it is crucial for us to extend and enrich a conception of moral ideals within professions. Otherwise, we play the logic of failure and risk losing those features of professions most capable of making work good (personally and morally).

The Challenge of Good Work

People are attracted to professions for a variety of reasons: the hope of higher pay and a better standard of living, job security and stability even in difficult economic times, a desire to serve others and to make the world a better place to live. Professions offer the promise of good work, a career that is rewarding financially and spiritually (in the broadest sense of the word), allowing people to more fully develop their physical and intellectual skills, to pursue self-actualization and fulfillment. Nevertheless, these lofty goals are not sufficient deterrents to bad behavior. There are numerous stories in the daily news which chronicle the unethical behaviors of people on the job. Today, it is about a university dean who allegedly misappropriated thousands of dollars of federal grants intended to promote children's education, and used the funds instead to purchase personal property and support a lavish lifestyle. Yesterday, it was a report of the disbarment of two attorneys, charged with defrauding their clients out of millions of dollars. Last week, the stories involved mortgage loan administrators who deceptively encouraged persons to take out home loans that they could not afford. There is no shortage of news accounts of professional misdeeds: the politician who accepted inappropriate gifts from lobbyists; the research biologist who falsified data so that it would more closely approximate a corporation's expectations; the journalist who fabricated news accounts, including information from "eyewitnesses" in hope of receiving higher pay and recognition. The frequency of these incidents and the incredible harm that they do, both to individuals and society as a whole, raise a number of perplexing questions. Do the processes by which people become professionals serve to make good workers? How can we do a better job of making professions good?

These questions challenge our concept of "good work," which obviously has two meanings: the first having to do with specialized knowledge, expertise, and professional skills; the second dealing with socially acceptable, morally good behavior. These two senses of good work are indicative of two crucial decisions that persons must make when choosing a profession: "What line of work shall I pursue?" and, "How committed am I to this profession?" Indeed, throughout one's working life the answers to these two questions may change several times. These are difficult questions and we have already seen how personal values and institutional structures can influence how persons respond to them. Moreover, *Conjectures* certainly contains narratives of Merton's own struggles to answer these questions.[31] In responding to these questions, people often rely on a sense of direction, a "moral compass." To be sure, this moral compass develops gradually throughout a person's life and it is the result of many social interactions. It undoubtedly changes over time and it is subject to strong polar influences that arise in a variety of contexts. Merton speaks of changes in his own "inner climate" in passages of *Conjectures* and reflects on his own "writing career" which he self-mockingly refers to as a "beautifully stupid fiction."[32] We all struggle with these questions, even Trappist monks.

In the book, *Making Good: How Young People Cope with Moral Dilemmas at Work*, researchers including Wendy Fischman and Howard Gardner report the results of Harvard University's long-term study into issues of "good work."[33] Their study explores the meaning of being an ethical professional in a given field; hence, it combines both senses of "good" mentioned above. They focus on three different professions: journalism, genetics, and theater, referring to these professions as "domains." A domain encompasses the central mission and core goals of a profession which have evolved over time. Participants in their research ranged in age from fifteen to thirty-five, divided into categories of newcomers or veterans depending on their work experience. The researchers asked participants to respond to questions about ethical issues that persons in these domains encounter, and the results shed fascinating light on what considerations people take into account when navigating difficult situations. The task of the research was to find patterns in the participants' responses which might lead to identification of constituents of good work, and hence to gain insight into those things which are relevant for "making good"—both professionally and ethically—the world of work. The investigation reveals how aspiring and seasoned professionals respond to people and conditions (particularly powerful market forces) that influence their work-lives, their perceptions of changes that are taking place in their professions, and perhaps most importantly, their hopes and fears, which influence the moves they make when faced with ethical dilemmas.

Of note in this investigation is the concept of a "well aligned" domain. As described by the authors, a well-aligned profession is one in which a majority of persons in vocation want the same things or are guided by similar goals and similar values. Professions are not always well-aligned, and the institutional forces we have discussed are capable of oscillating professions in and out of alignment. Without doubt, the alignment of a profession can be a desirable thing, and individuals may be attracted to domains that are well-aligned due to a fit between personal aspirations and the acknowledged values of a profession. People often speak of a "fit" between their self-identity and their vocational choice. Merton speaks of his own experience in *Conjectures*. However, alignment may often be temporary and sometimes undesirable—for example, when market conditions or economic performances become more important than other values.

The concept of domains captures the central purpose of a profession, which develops over time and changes only gradually. Corresponding to domains there are "fields," which consist of the institutions and organizations that constitute a domain. As we have seen, it is in the context of a field that a person, as an autonomous self (a web of desires, experiences, relationships, and personal values) seeks employment and fulfillment; the institutions, corporations, professional organizations, licensing agencies, and other members of a field provide the context and milieu in which persons operate in their professional roles. The research from this Harvard study brings to light factors that influence and differentiate persons as they move through the fields which map their respective domains. These factors include their attitudes toward work, senses of responsibility, private reflections on their respective domains, uneven experiences of their given fields, and varying ethical sensitivities. This study teases out the values indicative of the maturity of veterans in a given domain, the idealism often mixed with moral insensitivity of youth aspiring to rise in a given profession, and for both groups, their high expectations contrasted by frustrations with moral ambiguities.

Consider persons committed to the acting profession, specifically theater (small stages and large ones, but not including television or film). As a profession, acting in the theater certainly has different educational requirements than other domains like journalism and genetics. In this domain, achieving success can be more a matter of natural talent and experience combined with collaboration with others than a matter of education. Although competition for roles can be very intense, persons who choose this profession view the theater as a "communal adventure" (some refer to it as "church" for them) and a collective effort that requires much cooperation and compromise on the part of its devotees. Veterans of this domain are highly motivated by a passion for their work. From the point of view of a majority of actors, the mission of this domain, the purpose of the theater, is to give society an image of itself. Beyond mere entertainment, the veterans see theater as serving as a means of social change, a catalyst for individual and collective "spiritual" enlightenment, a space and a context in which revelations of truths about oneself and society can be explored. Veteran actors who participated in this research expressed a large degree of confidence in their abilities, combined with a very strong sense of responsibility to self. In their responses, they discussed the emotional and physical tolls of this career. Though the salary range for theater actors is not very high and is tempered by periodic unemployment—hence the necessity of working other, often menial, jobs—they have come to see these difficulties as equipping them with a deep inner strength that can further contribute to their acting abilities.

Their concerns about the future of the theater notwithstanding, they also possessed a very positive outlook on the domain.

Young actors typically described themselves as very imaginative and often mentioned a desire to perform going back to early childhood. Many of them expressed their attraction to this profession in fateful terms: they "could not help choosing" acting, they have a sense of predestination to a theatrical career, a submission to a calling. The researchers saw in these young people heightened senses of self-awareness and self-importance too (a little bit of egoism), but they also seemed to have a high view of responsibility to others and particularly to the audience, though not necessarily to the domain itself. Pressures from authority figures, tensions of working in collaboration with others, and quandaries arising from the need to earn money versus the desire to maintain a deep sense of personal integrity, are only a few of the ethical dilemmas faced by young aspiring actors. In this domain as in many others, market forces have a huge impact on the profession, and young actors often face the temptation of compromising personal values for career advancement.

In contrast to theater, the domain of science has changed dramatically over the past fifty years. Incredible expansion in genetics research is merely one example of progress and opportunities now possible. To be sure, influences of market forces and the power of capital are dramatically present in science, as clearly evident in the emergence of the biotech industry. Many of these developments have radically changed the public's image of the scientist. But these advances have also changed how education in science takes place. The current trend from education to employment demands that one's choice of a career in science take place at quite a young age. Prior to college, intensive high school preparation puts one on a path toward a career in the biological sciences. To be a professional in the domain of genetics requires a Ph.D. and biomedical training, easily committing a person to over eight years of graduate school education. The combination of one's academic work, experience, and postdoctoral fellowships is intended to transition one into the profession with choices ranging from academic to corporate career tracks. So the amount of knowledge and extremely high level of required skills necessitates that one should begin at a young age to train for a career in this branch of science.

Veteran geneticists have been witnesses to unparalleled changes to the profession in the past fifty years. They are deeply aware of the numerous ethical and social issues that arise within their domain. They are no doubt guided by the longstanding medical principle of non-maleficence, the solemn vow "to do no harm" expressed in the Hippocratic Oath. However, there is little evidence from the veterans that it is possible to find much consensus on how to resolve these complex issues. They even show little agreement about who ought to have the authority to do so. These veterans extol truth and integrity as values of the highest importance for the profession and for their individual careers. Additionally, they possess a strong sense of service to others through their profession. However, many of these geneticists believe that others, not themselves, should determine the "uses of science."

Consequently, although they find their work very rewarding and prospects numerous, the veteran geneticists also face serious ethical challenges. Opportunities abound for exploiting people, particularly graduate students engaged in assisting research. There are numerous temptations to do hasty, less careful work in an effort to speed up production and publications. Some scientists express a reluctance to share information and resources with colleagues due to distrust of others, and the belief (sometimes justified) that data or ideas will be inappropriately used or stolen. In addition, there is fierce competition for grants and research funding. Many of these challenges spring from pressures of the market and its quest for huge profits. The choice between the pursuit of new discoveries or the replication of research results (the latter being so important to science) is the source of much tension, and pressures arise from increased academic and corporate collaboration. The veterans struggle on many levels between their ideals for the advancement of science and the realities of the daily marketplace. There is no doubt that organizational structures and institutional contexts have huge influences over these professionals, making this domain fraught with ethical conflicts and moral distress.

Perhaps not surprisingly then, mentoring is highly important in this domain and it takes place in a very structured manner. The profession of genetics, unlike other professions, has no "orphans" in the sense of that vast in-between stage where one is virtually abandoned to oneself, no longer a newcomer but nowhere near a veteran. In this domain, the neophytes work closely with the veterans, sometimes for years, and their careers are shaped by this close collaboration. Thus, one aspect which makes this profession unique is the emphasis placed on teaching and mentoring, which results in a kind of soft paternalism that has the side-effect of taking away some of the moral freedom of younger professionals. Schmidt argues that the "weeding out" process of education and training—the massive elimination of persons who, for various reasons, do not "measure up" to the established requirements—has a strong effect on the ideological transformation leading up to graduation and employment.[34]

There is great pressure on everyone in this profession to follow institutional guidelines, strictly adhere to specific standards, and toe the organizational line. Moreover, young people who are attracted to this profession face intense individual competition from the very beginning. Internationally recognized science talent searches motivate many youth with a desire for recognition and scholarship funding, often challenging their moral senses of truth and honesty. Hence in this domain, the role of teachers and the importance of mentoring for a young scientist are decidedly important and influential; the complexity of relationships across the field combined with temptations of fortune and power make it necessary to have good guidance.

Many young scholars in this profession express the pursuit of excellence as their personal ideal, coupled with a palpable motivation to acquire material prosperity and to succeed at all costs. The young scientists are quickly introduced to the tension between personal versus professional morality, and their survival in the profession often depends on a careful balance between competition and integrity. Even though they strongly express support for a professional code of ethics, admittedly, sometimes the desire to win in a highly competitive scientific environment will trump the consciences of the young scientists. Nevertheless, the students are also quite adept at justifying poor moral choices: one student, who confessed to falsifying methodological information in a research competition stated, "but I thought that it [the act of cheating] was fair because I think that I deserved the recognition that other people did that worked just as hard if not less than I did."[35] So, in spite of their expressions of high moral ideals and the striving for excellence, young scientists may betray a willingness to compromise their values in pursuit of their best possible education and for the prospect of professional success. Overall they do exhibit a strong sense of responsibility, according to the researchers, but within a context of numerous mixed motives.

Moreover, they also attribute responsibility to others in a very strong way. Having not exercised a great deal of moral freedom in their early careers, they are quick to shift moral responsibility to others, both to the veteran professionals and to society. In their responses, one young professional stated the belief that society—not the profession—is responsible for how new biotechnology is developed and used. This attitude stands in stark contrast to other professionals, like journalists, who attributed responsibility for the profession only to those inside of it. The geneticists believe that their responsibilities and the accompanying "gray areas" of their profession will grow much larger in the future. Despite the uniqueness of their domain, the geneticists face some difficulties common with other professionals. They express concerns over a lack of power to act in complex situations. They also share the belief that there is little time for those just entering the profession to thoughtfully consider ethical issues. As Merton describes in *Conjectures*, one slowly becomes bound by pragmatic considerations of every urgency until one finally loses perspective and one's sense of values. Without a relevant context in which to contemplate the significance of actions and consequences, life becomes "erratic, arbitrary and insignificant."[36] Consequently, some of these young professionals decide that these formidable challenges are simply too great and they choose to leave the profession.

Journalism presents some of the most tenacious and intricate ethical tensions. The importance of a free press to democracy can hardly be overstated. Threats to a free press are many and come from a wide variety of directions. One could give a history of this domain beginning with newspapers, for example, and discuss the emergence of new forms of media, competition between media outlets, and the forces of market capitalism on the entire domain. A similar narrative could be given of the field, which would include the emergence of professional organizations, associations, and the development of ethical codes of conduct designed to serve as standards for persons in this profession. Of the three professions studied by the researchers, journalism demonstrated the widest variation of responses and the least amount of alignment within the profession. Discussions with veterans in this profession yielded quite interesting results. Guided by a strong desire to uncover facts and discover truths about situations, veteran journalists expressed a keen sense of unity with others (most reminiscent of Singer's "point of view of the universe" but not completely unlike Merton's view) which allow them to hold firm beliefs about their objectives. They combine their interest in current and historical fact-finding with unique abilities to communicate effectively and clearly. Not surprisingly then, three purposes of the domain seem to emerge from discussions with veterans of this profession. First, they express a strong desire to communicate relevant knowledge to an audience, guiding choices of what to cover and how best to present news information. Second, they exhibit a firm commitment to democratic values, that is, providing information which can lead to informed debate and the free exchange of ideas. Third, and perhaps most interesting, these veteran journalists see their work as *empowering* both individuals and society, particularly persons who might be marginalized such as the poor and minorities. A balance of truth, fairness, and accuracy, these values are at the core of the profession for the veterans. Consequently, the veterans see specific and formidable challenges to the future of the domain, not the least of which are the forces of the marketplace and corporate capitalism that have greater influence over the institutions and organizations which constitute their field.

Perhaps not surprisingly, young journalists have a much different view of the domain than their veteran counterparts. For the purposes of this research, young journalists were identified as high school students and college journalism majors, who typically work for small school-based newspapers or as interns. Quite often, these young people are attracted to the domain through recognition of their ability to write and communicate effectively. As aspiring journalists, their sense of purpose is grounded on two goals: first, to discuss issues of concern to their fellow classmates; and second, to provide news and stories that will have a positive affect on their readers. Ranking the value of responsibility to peers very highly, young journalists indicated that they are reluctant to publish stories that might cause uneasiness or distress in their communities. This attitude is very different from their veteran counterparts who express commitment to personal integrity, truth, and the domain much more highly, and who have less concern about disturbing the general tranquility of the community when the pursuit of truth is at stake. For these young workers, tensions on the job come from external conflicts with those in authority such as principals, administrators, and parents, and internal conflicts over their own senses of personal integrity and idealism colliding with a sense of respect for authority and responsibility to others. While they have sought to obey the demands of administrators and teachers, the students have also striven to maintain the integrity of their values in the face of resistance from authority figures and peers.

A provocative aspect of this domain lies between the veterans and the students: the young professionals. While also acknowledging a sense of responsibility to the community and to readers, young professional journalists stress the importance of accuracy in their reporting. A profound sense of fairness seems to underlie much of their moral reasoning. Interestingly, these young professionals are very critical of graduate education concerning ethical issues. They claim that although "J-school" gave many opportunities for consideration of ethical issues, it actually did little to prepare them for the moral dilemmas that occur routinely in the daily life of a professional. In particular, they note the absence of a collegiality that was present in their prior experiences, having discovered that they are now engaged in an intense competition with current peers. Moreover, the moral values of truth and integrity often come into conflict for these members of the profession because they are faced with the necessity of following orders and pressures to conform at the risk of losing one's career at the very start. The young professionals acknowledge a very high degree of conflict between the values to which they aspire and the methods that they are called on to use in order to pursue and develop news information. They are especially sensitive to pressures from editors, producers, and administrators to embellish stories and sensationalize accounts. Under pressure from their editors, compelled by the fear of losing a job, sometimes young journalists give in to these demands. Other times, they develop resistance strategies which circumvent these demands and allow them to maintain their sense of integrity and credibility. Many of these young professionals express a high measure of confidence in their own good intentions, and share a belief that, "I will be different when I'm the boss." Hence, a delicate balance arises between compromise and career, between personal integrity and professional ambition.

It would seem from this research that young professionals are the most vulnerable ones, either too willing to compromise or unsure about how to react to challenges in the profession. To their credit, they are explicitly concerned with ethical issues. They seem deeply troubled by disconnects between their ideals and the routine or daily practices of their profession. For many of these young people, the result is a loss of the meaning of work and a sense of self-fulfillment or satisfaction from performing a job well done. To this extent, the future of the profession is at stake, for young journalists represent the future of the domain yet find themselves torn between trading their moral compass for a roadmap to quick success or evading the alienation of their work by abandoning the profession for some other career.

Enlightening aspects of this research include the respondents' conceptions of "good work," the notion of vocation as "a calling," and the relationship between work and self-identity. For veterans established in their chosen professions, the moral North Star most often appears as responsibility and loyalty to the domain. With long-standing careers to protect (given the difficulty of changing professions late in life), veterans show the good and bad influences of what Schmidt calls, "disciplined minds." For young professionals, however, their moral compasses seem to spin between responsibilities to self and loyalty to one's closest peers. The matrix of self-identity and career choice provides the context in which many conflicts between responsibilities arise: duties to self, to authority figures, to the field and the domain, and to society as a whole. Here the language games come to the fore, aided by the ethical theories like utilitarianism and deontology, to construct justifications for attributions of praise and guilt. It is also in this context that the shifting and ascribing of responsibilities to others takes place, both as the desire to hold someone else responsible for the milieu in which ethical dilemmas arise and the insinuation that others outside the profession are responsible for the mission and values of the domain.

It is also noteworthy from this study that some values do not seem to be domain- or context-sensitive. Honesty and integrity, commitment, and quality of work are values ranked very highly by all participants. Moreover, recognition of the forces of capital and the power of the marketplace seem to be acknowledged by professionals young and old. But the differences between age groups in their responses to questions of moral values in the professions lead the authors to posit several factors contributing to a sense of "good work." First, the centrality of a long-standing value system; that is, a set of fundamental beliefs and moral values deeply held by an individual, whether originating from family, religious, or other personal associations. When faced with an ethical dilemma many people rely upon values inculcated in them through their religious or familial upbringing. Moreover, when individuals enter the workplace, they typically bring these value systems with them into the domain.

Another factor contributing to a sense of "good work" is the tremendous influence of one's peers. Both the selection and closeness of association with peers can shape an aspiration for high ethical ideals or an acceptance of low moral standards. Peers help shape one's self-image and can have a tremendous magnetic pull on one's individual moral compass. Peers also contribute to one's interpretation and assimilation of pivotal experiences, like one's educational and professional development. These factors can have a decided impact on the formation of one's ethical values. Levels of trust (as we have noted, so important to professions) and willingness to cooperate with others are just a few of the values that can be shaped by past experiences and interaction with peers, which going forward can influence the ethical trajectory of one's career.

Additionally, we have stressed, and the research reinforces, the view that institutional milieu is significant for understanding the context in which ethical and unethical choices are made. In *My Job, My Self* author Al Gini notes, "The general climate and culture of the workplace indelibly mark us for life. Work is the means by which we form our character and complete ourselves as persons."[37] Corporations and firms have their own ethical climates, and the moral atmosphere in which one works affects individual workers from the boardroom to the back door. Eric Mount explains how the organization of work can define not only rules for success but also virtues; in the words of Michael Maccoby, "any organization of work . . . can be described as a psychostructure that selects and molds character."[38] The researchers in this Harvard study argue that institutions and organizations can support healthy and growing professionals by giving periodic ethical "booster shots" to help protect them from various temptations and pressures as they develop from neophytes to veterans.

While factors identified by the Harvard researchers are not intended to stipulate the necessary and sufficient conditions of good work, they do serve as indicators or symptoms of those features that one should consider in the choice of how not only to make a living but also to make a life worth living. In *Disciplined Minds*, Jeff Schmidt argues that,

> the hidden root of much career dissatisfaction is the professional's lack of control over the 'political' component of his or her work. Today's disillusioned professionals entered their fields expecting to do work that would 'make a difference' in the world and add meaning to their lives. In fact, professional education and employment push people to accept a role in which they do not make a significant difference.[39]

For any professional domain (not just these) to continue attracting the brightest and best persons, issues of trust, integrity, and other moral concerns must continually be addressed. Otherwise, the danger arises that either the cognitive dissonance between personal values and daily practices will drive people away from vocations or, remaining there, they will become so ethically hard-hearted that the possibility of finding "good work" will become even more difficult for future generations.

What do we learn from listening to both the veterans and the young people entering these three professions? What is the role of education? How should it function in equipping young professionals to face the difficult ethical choices arising in these domains? In response, the researchers state,

> Chief among [the findings of this research] is our discovery that younger workers are faced with conflicts for which they have little guidance: they must wrestle with these, reach a solution, and live with the consequences. In struggling with these conflicts, they are loath to pass judgment on others; and they believe, in turn, that they ought to be given latitude to do what they feel is right.[40]

Young people in all of these professions show great sensitivity to ethical issues and strong senses of personal integrity. Though often idealistic, they seem aware of the threats to good work and demonstrate a desire to act ethically even in difficult situations. Yet, simultaneously, they are highly self-motivated and concerned about their opportunities for career advancement in light of intense competition and powerful market forces. Ethical dilemmas occur in all occupations, and these young professionals exhibit a determination to mark out their moral freedom in the context of their own individuality and pursuit of self-interests. The moral freedom that they struggle to articulate and exemplify in their actions seems to be a curious blend of relativism and egoism. While acknowledging the rules, these young professionals desire the moral freedom to interpret the rules whenever they see fit, nevertheless wanting to believe that their own twisting of the rules is both temporary and benign. To this extent, these young people seem to typify many of the beliefs about the nature of morality apparently prominent in American pop-culture today. Indeed, many Americans give the impression of being indifferent about ethics education, presumably under the assumptions that a) moral intuitions are innate or at most, instilled in one at a very early age, and b) that ethics education may only serve to confuse rather than to clarify one's moral intuitions.

The Harvard research project also reveals how young people struggle to balance their personal interests and desires in relation to their talents and goals. While the sense of personal responsibility may vary among participants, this study reveals how strong the temptations are to be unethical once entering the workforce. It also shows how passionately youth can believe themselves to be honest at heart, while at the same time engaging in dishonest means to achieve their professional goals. David Callahan reflects on ethical issues confronting young professionals in his recent book, *The Cheating Culture*, claiming,

> Fabrications by journalists (for example) are nothing new nor are conflicts of interest in the media. But while there is no hard evidence that misconduct in journalism has increased in recent years, there are plenty of reasons to think that journalists are facing new pressures on their integrity that stem from a greater focus on the bottom line and bigger pay disparities.[41]

Hence, we can glean from this Harvard research project the subtle markings of a downward ethical slide: how the push to be successful and establish oneself in a career often sets the stage for an intense conflict between professional ethics and private morality, and how institutional structures limit the ability of individuals to exercise freedom in moral decision-making. In the midst of such conflicting responsibilities, compromises seem not only inevitable but also notoriously difficult to navigate.

If professional ethics is to avoid the oxymoron label, which is often attached to concepts like "business ethics," veterans of professions and educators alike must work together to bring about positive changes in professional domains. It should not surprise us that young people cope with moral dilemmas at work in much the same way as they do other ethical conflicts: by understanding how to apply moral values to situations, by being willing to come forward and discuss issues, and by following the positive examples of peers and mentors. By acknowledging difficult ethical dilemmas in every domain, recognizing differences in perspectives and skill-sets from neophytes to veterans, and by affirming the centrality of critical reflection on moral values in professional life at every level, there is a much greater chance of success in "making good" the potential of professional life.

There is an insightful connection between the research participants of this Harvard study and Merton's experience in leading the novices. From 1951 to 1955 Merton served as Master of Scholastics, the teacher of students preparing for priesthood, and from 1955 through 1965 Merton was Master of Novices, in effect a manager of personnel aspiring to full membership in the Order. In several passages of *Conjectures*, Merton discusses his experiences and observations in leading the novices. Novices are trained, he mentions, to "do everything as if the abbot is watching you." Sometimes priests get upset, according to Merton, over deeds which are good but nevertheless violate some tiny detail of a code of observance. He marvels that, when faced with a choice between an act of compassion and a violation of "punctilious usage," the novices will often choose to act according to the latter. After all, he seems to scoff, violating the code would give them far more guilt.[42] This is not unlike the professionals in the Harvard study, nor is it dissimilar from managers and employees in the daily workplace. How often does the opportunity of an act of charity or compassion get pushed aside for the security of following standard procedures or the code of ethics? The pressure to conform to institutional requirements, to capitulate to organizational hierarchy, and to loyally (if not blindly) follow ordinary procedures can be greater than the desire to follow the demands of compassion.

In addition to struggles with institutional pressures, I believe the professionals in the Harvard study and the novices under Merton's tutelage are similar in their search for self-identity. Ideally, one's vocation, whether priest or plumber, says something about who one is — this is what I do, this is who I am. As Al Gini has noted, one's work can be an indication and constituent of one's self-identity. This seems particularly true for professions because of the relative stability and potential of a long-term career; unlike someone who may change jobs many times and work in a variety of fields, professionals may change employers or locations but tend to do similar tasks. A danger, of course, is that one over-identifies with one's vocation, an acute problem for "workaholics" (as many professionals can be) and for any line of work that requires intensive education and training, long hours, and monotonous routines. Recall the bad faith of Sartre's waiter. The importance of dialectic and contemplation is to serve as a safeguard against over-identification of self with work. Losing one's self-identity in work is simply another way in which we become irresponsible by artificially separating one's self from others. Professions are made for people, not people for professions. It has become a cliché, "be yourself," but it seems to be one of Merton's insights into his own calling and his relationship with institutional hierarchy; it is one thing that he could not teach the novices, but could only serve as a guide. We, too, can learn from his guidance.

Chapter Four

Professional Ethics and Moral Imagination

Professional life offers many advantages to those who pursue it. In the long, sordid history of human labor the concept of a profession, of being a professional, is relatively new. The expansion of this concept as a category of labor has increased dramatically in the last seventy years. Professions are attractive precisely because they promise a variety of benefits to those who pursue them. But we have also seen that professional life is fraught with difficulties. Its benefits and advantages come with a cost. We have analyzed a few of the most egregious perils of professional life. The fragmentation of the self into a variety of roles can have the effect of ripping one's personal moral intuitions from one's professional obligations. Moreover, institutions have ways of diminishing our moral freedom and creativity through our participation in them. The result is that we lose confidence and hope that work can be good, both in terms of productivity and in terms of morality.

Ethics Training and Habituating the Good

In an earlier discussion of Aristotle's view of ethics, I mentioned a common adage in many gyms. This saying, like the familiar "No pain, no gain" slogan found in so many workout rooms, was posted in the exercise facility at our university. It read, "It is hard to do a great thing suddenly." I like that message because it reminds me of Aristotle's view on virtue. It would have been ridiculous for me, on the first day I stumbled into the gym from a sedentary lifestyle, to attempt to run for any length of time on a treadmill or to aggressively use any of the other equipment. Such acts at the time would likely have required immediate medical attention! However, over time, with dedication and perseverance (and sometimes, yes, pain was involved) I began to get in better physical condition. I could not have achieved any of these things on my first visit, not even within the first months. One year later however, it was a much different story.

Such is the view of Aristotle's theory of ethics. Another example of language shaping our experience, given that words are laden with value judgments: When we hear the word "habit" we tend to think of a negative connotation; habits are things to be broken. Aristotle viewed habits not as negative, but as positive behavior patterns. Recall that Aristotle suggests that we can reason our way to virtue, we can know that something is good by recognizing that it occupies a middle ground between two extremes: a lack of virtue or goodness on one hand and an excess on the other hand. For Aristotle, we can discern that courage is a virtue, that it is good, precisely because it occupies a sort of middle ground between a lack of courage on one hand (this would be "cowardice") and an excess of it (we might call it "foolhardiness") on the other hand. Having this knowledge about virtue, however, is not enough for Aristotle. We must live it out in our everyday lives. We do that by habituating ourselves to act virtuously. This involves training and habituating ourselves to the Good.

Years ago, I would teach a course in the summer at Fort Knox, not far from Gethsemani, the very military base that Merton often speaks of in his writing. In the heat and humidity of the late summer afternoon, soldiers would be going through their "basic training" routines, in full combat gear and carrying heavy backpacks. Even on rainy days they would be there, crawling through the mud and under barbed wire while mortar shells and artillery rounds shook the entire environment. Watching from the classroom at the barracks, I was glad that I had chosen my profession! Why were they doing these things, especially on such muggy days and in difficult circumstances? The answer is simple: one must become acclimated to combat conditions in order to live and be successful in those types of situations. An army could not function as such if we merely distributed weapons to volunteers and wished them good luck as we bid them farewell to the battleground. It is not enough to have the finest equipment or the best plans. The training exercises serve the purpose of habituating the right actions in difficult circumstances.

Merton would probably not like this analogy; the training in effect makes a game of it, like playing war. In *Conjectures of a Guilty Bystander*, he denounces the connection between game theory and actual war. "In our society everything, in fact, is a game," Merton quips and then adds,

> but the real excitement of the game comes from the suspension of conscience. In all play, one has to prescind from real conditions . . . the need for a massive suspension of conscience, a total irresponsibility.[1]

Given his stance on war and military society, I seriously doubt that Merton would approve my use of this example. However, I use it because, like that of regularly visiting the gym, it supports an important point about training and habituating oneself to pursue the good. So, I can accept his potential criticism, yet tease out the implications of "making a game of it" and of the "suspension of conscience" because I believe Merton has made a very astute observation that has implications for professional ethics. We would like to believe that, ideally, averting moral failure and resisting poor choices could simply be a matter of receiving the proper training. With the right amount of education and simulation, moral pitfalls could be avoided and good behavior lionized. However, rather than preparing one for the sorts of dilemmas one will confront on the job, can it become a sort of game? Rather than priming oneself with moral sensitivity to deal with issues, can it become an occasion for the suspension of conscience? Can ethics training and education accomplish the lofty task that they are assigned?

Similar to Plato's question in several of his dialogues as to whether virtue can be taught, one might skeptically raise the question, "Can persons really be trained to act ethically at work?" Without question, ethics training in professions and on the job has increased dramatically in recent years. On the job, training may be for occasional short periods of time. In a profession, it may be a semester-long course or more during one's education and then "continuing education credits" afterwards. In either case, the usual structure of the training follows the same typical pattern. One begins with a discussion of the importance of ethics to the profession or the organization, spelling out the justification and the need for focusing on ethical issues in this context. This is frequently followed by a description of several moral theories, including and in similar fashion to the beginning of this book. The importance of the theoretical perspectives to moral reasoning and the exercise of sound judgment are explained, justifying a philosophical approach to the subject. Revisions, alternatives, and conflicting viewpoints within each theory may be covered to some degree, in order to show that none of them are sufficiently comprehensive or persuasive to elicit the satisfaction of everyone. The next step in the training is to cover one or more decision-making paradigms. There are many of these paradigms available, authors and professors often make up their own. Sometimes the first letter of the word for each step is used to spell out an acronym for the process, so some of the decision models may have funny names like "P.L.P.S.," or one of my favorites, "D.I.S.O.R.D.E.R."[2] Some models may have four steps, other models may have eight; I know of one model with four different categories of issues which has a total of twenty-eight questions to consider (not a model for quick decisions!). Some professional organizations use their own decision-making models, and a few corporations have developed guidelines or rubrics for their employees to follow.

The next step of ethics training involves combining the use of a given decision-making model with the ethical theories one has been supplied with, to produce a well-articulated justification to a selected ethical issue. The rubric provides appropriate questions one ought to ask when confronted with a problem and the theories provide perspectives from which to evaluate responses to those questions. The paradigm tells you *what* you ought to be thinking about, the theories tell *how* you should be thinking about it. Using the decision-making model in combination with the moral theories ideally generates a *resolution* (one should hesitate to say *solution*, since it implies only one correct answer) to a particular moral problem, and provides one with reasons to defend that resolution. With this preparatory work now complete, the next step of ethics training involves the application of this method to specific cases, the types of scenarios a professional might encounter on the job. Training in professional ethics, like the soldiers going through their drills, involves habituating oneself to making good decisions and taking right actions in difficult situations.

This is the point where I believe Merton's observation about game-playing has merit. Following this method of ethics training, whether the annual ritualized one in an office setting or the semester-long one in an academic setting, going through these procedures becomes a kind of game. There are both good and bad reasons for structuring ethics training in this game-like fashion. Learning to apply the insights of moral theories through use of decision-making rubrics is very useful. Just being mindful of a decision-making model can be extremely helpful when confronted with an ethical dilemma; though not providing one with ready-made answers, it does inform one of the important considerations which should influence any decision: applicable laws, rights, potential consequences, relevant stakeholders, etc. Moreover, when employing this process to a case study in one's profession, the classroom setting provides a neutral atmosphere in which professionals can explore various options and experiment with outcomes and justifications in a relatively non-consequential environment. These features are good; this *is* basic ethics training. Nevertheless, there are shortcomings of this process, particularly the way in which decision-making can become routinized and scripted by the process, and the way in which students or employees can begin to simply "play the game" as Merton suggests. Let us examine these issues.

There are at least two problems that follow from an ethical decision-making process which becomes ritualized and scripted. First is the obvious opportunity for bad faith to undermine the intent of the training. One may simply become conditioned to follow each step of the method in a procedural fashion, effectively removing considerations of conscience from the equation, to which Merton alluded. The danger of this "suspension of conscience" is the possibility that philosophically defensible or institutionally sanctioned resolutions might nevertheless result in irresponsible behavior. A routinized way of decision-making sets one up for the logic of failure because it allows one to go through the process glibly or barely awake, not considering the existential import or full range of contextual features that are part of the situation.

The second problem with a ritualized decision-making process is rooted in the structure of the ethics training. Though seldom recognized or analyzed, components of this method of decision-making can show a degree of evaluative bias. This bias may be intentionally or unintentionally present in various elements of the training program. Consider the narrative structure of cases, for example. Relatively short scenarios of ethical dilemmas are the heart of the case-study approach to ethics training. These narratives place professionals in situations of incompatible duties, competing values, conflicts of interest, and the like. The form and structure of these narratives are rarely scrutinized however. Bioethicist and philosopher Robert Veatch has authored many such cases, specific to nursing, physicians, and allied health professionals.[3] Case study narratives usually begin with the introduction of a character, often the healthcare professional, followed by a description of a patient and of the circumstances that give rise to an ethical dilemma. Enough information is given to set up the scenario but the case is left open-ended for readers to engage in the decision-making process. However, in his book *A Philosophical Disease*, fellow bioethicist and philosopher Carl Elliott insists that we should look deeper than the point of the story, to that which is unspoken. He recounts the arguments of twentieth-century philosopher Ludwig Wittgenstein, whose perspectives on language and meaning parallel the "traditional" and "postmodern" views of language that I articulated in the first chapter. Wittgenstein's earliest view was that language functions to represent reality. Words picture actual facts about the world, such that the logical relations between words are similar to the logical relations between things. Later in his career, however, Wittgenstein rejected this early view on the recognition that our use of language is much messier and more complex than merely representing reality. In this spirit of Wittgenstein's later view, Elliott highlights the work of Tod Chambers, who argues that a case study does not merely picture a given reality, nor does it represent features of a situation in a straightforward way. Rather, more deeply, the style of writing present in a case reveals the philosophical views of the bioethicist authoring them. Following Chambers, Elliott argues that in his cases, "Veatch doesn't simply give us a context for the moral problem; he creates a world."[4] He creates a hostile urban world in his narratives, and environment in which no one can be trusted and each person must live according to their own private moral code. "Veatch's characters don't trust the authorities," says Elliott, "they must go outside the law for help . . . they cannot rely on conventional morality."[5] He goes on to explain,

> As with Veatch's case narrative, says Chambers, so it is with his moral theory. Veatch's objective is to convince his readers to abandon ethics based on professional codes and opt instead for a contractarian approach, with individual doctors and patients coming to mutually agreed-upon understandings. The cold, cynical world Veatch constructs in his case narrative reinforces the need for such contracts in such a world we should not assume that anyone can be trusted.[6]

Elliott points out that the importance of this realization is not to persuade bioethicists to write their cases more objectively, but simply to acknowledge that cases have particular moral attitudes and perspectives built into the very fabric of the narrative.

Hence, the importance of Merton's comment applied to this issue is the recognition that the process of the training itself conditions one to interpret and resolve ethical conflicts in a very narrow way, a way that can "suspend the conscience" and allow one to participate in a kind of "mass immorality" justified by the rules of the ethics training game. "What is problematic," states Elliott, "is not that narrative style communicates a personal moral vision, but that it packages a personal moral vision in the surface wrapping of objectivity."[7] Naïvely, cases may seem to be merely laying out the facts, but students and employees become conditioned by the unspoken aspects of ethics training to see and respond to ethical dilemmas in particular ways that may not be welcome or intended. Ethics education in this case seems to take on the nature of scripted outcomes and routine following of approved formulas. Rather than increasing one's moral sensitivity and empowering a person's moral acuity, this sort of process could have the opposite effect of dulling the conscience and weakening one's perceptiveness.

Both of these ways of scripting the process of ethics training contribute to the second shortcoming mentioned above, the way in which students and employees may simply play the game of ethical reflection. A brief incident at the beginning of my teaching career made me vividly aware of this point. After discussing a relatively simple case (the case of the cheating classmate mentioned earlier), class was dismissed. On the way out, a student innocently said to me, "Well, that's the conclusion which I came to, but it is not what I would do in real life." At that moment I realized that—even though I explicitly assure students that I have little interest in which resolution they come to, but place great emphasis on how they come to it—students will articulate the answers that they believe the instructor wants to hear. Likewise, employees will write in the space provided (or click on the box of the online quiz) the resolution which they have been conditioned to recognize as the organization's preference. Students and professionals "play the game." The game is played by giving one answer for the professor or boss in order to pass the training successfully, while knowing that in all likelihood they would not follow this course of action in a real-life situation.

I contend that ethics training is very important to professional life and it is useful in reasoning through moral dilemmas in the workplace. We are confronted by ethical conflicts on a daily basis. Some of them may be rather benign and we may come to address them in a routine sort of way; but others can be quite difficult, with irreversible consequences, and the task of deciding what to do in such situations can be agonizing. Equipping a person with knowledge of moral theories and decision-making models is a good method for establishing a baseline process of ethical consideration for professionals. This method can be an excellent way of habituating professionals to pursue the highest good. However, as Merton's criticism of "playing the game" reveals, ethics training alone is not a sufficient means to ensure good choices or right actions. Scripting resolutions to ethical dilemmas merely suspends the conscience and proceeds from that point on in bad faith. Allowing ourselves to be conditioned by the intentionally and unintentionally communicated values of an organization also suspends the conscience, creates an atmosphere of irresponsibility, and can lead to a "mass immorality" in which we are all satisfied because we comfort ourselves that we played by the rules. Going through a programmatic decision-making routine is not enough. Ethics training can be another form guilty bystanding.

Guided by Integrity versus Occupied with Compliance

It may seem surprising that in *Conjectures* Merton discusses the need for ethics training. "It is more then ever necessary for the individual to train himself or be training," writes Merton, "according to objective norms of the good, and learn to distinguish these from the purely pragmatic norms current in society."[8] Given his emphasis on self-knowledge and reasoned moral action, he does not believe that one should rely solely on organizations or even society to tell one the difference between right and wrong. Whenever we practice what he calls the "ethics of expediency" and focus our attention on efficiency and consequences, we become confused; we make mistakes in judgment because we vacillate between urgency and opportunity. What Merton is arguing for, this notion of training oneself, gives rise to a distinction between an inner veracity as opposed to an external conformity.

Merton's argument has important implications for professional ethics because his distinction highlights two very different approaches to promoting moral behavior. One approach emphasizes an *internal* process of searching and growth; the other route stresses *external* mechanisms for achieving conventionality. Harvard Business School professor Lynn Sharp Paine makes a similar argument and applies it to organizational management.[9] In the post-Enron era, companies have rapidly developed ethics programs. In many cases the government, regulatory, or professional agencies mandate these programs. Quite often, these programs are developed by legal counsel. Paine argues that such programs function from external, even punitive measures; they do not promote an internal motivation towards excellence. She maintains that fostering an ethical atmosphere in an organization cannot be accomplished merely from conformity to external norms developed to comply with legal requirements. Firms need a more comprehensive approach to create a climate that encourages exemplary behavior. Paine identifies the former as a "compliance approach" and the latter as an "integrity approach." An integrity-based approach, she argues, is the best way to emphasize managerial responsibility and to promote good decision-making.

Paine recounts some of the classic cases in business ethics, examples that highlight the myriad of ways in which organizations shape individuals' behavior. In the early 1990s, Sears Auto Centers created a plan that offered large incentives to local managers for increasing sales to customers having their cars serviced. However, executives did not clarify differences between preventive maintenance and unnecessary repairs. Overall sales increased and managers received large bonuses, but only because many customers paid for services that they did not actually need. Resulting litigation cost the company tens of millions of dollars. Another particularly egregious example from the late 1980s involved the Beech-Nut company, whose incoming executive discovered that its "100% pure" apple juice contained zero apple content. The juice was nothing more than sugar water with additional chemicals. Of course, the money saved on ingredients and processing costs allowed the company to have a twenty-five percent price advantage over competitors. However, when an employee of the company, a researcher at one of their laboratories, voiced concerns about the product, he was severely reprimanded for "not being a team player." In both of these cases, employees were following corporate guidelines and complying with demands of management, but with bad results. These are only two cases of many more, which illustrate the "logic of failure" built into compliance strategies.

According to Paine, employees often see compliance programs as thinly veiled protections for executives and senior managers. The annual ethics training program can be viewed by employees as nothing more than a form of liability protection. Not only does it fail to provide guidance for managers facing ethical conflicts, it does nothing to inspire exemplary behavior. Compliance programs do not invoke commitment to even the best worded corporate codes of ethics, much less support or help to develop moral imagination. To be sure, this is a result of their legal foundation; the law does not inspire human excellence, it simply provides the baseline for acceptable behavior and justifications for dealing with those who fall below it. "Managers who define ethics as legal compliance," Paine argues, "merely endorse a code of moral mediocrity for their organizations."[10] An integrity-based approach holds organizations to a more robust standard. It places organizational ethics in the hands of management, not legal counsel, and encourages formation of an atmosphere of shared accountability among all members. Corporate counsel may be involved in the design of a program and perhaps its implementation, but employees across all levels contribute to the process. Rather than attempting to contain unethical behavior through a variety of negative means, an integrity-based approach uses positive means to create an environment that supports ethically sound behavior.

When one considers the objectives, the methods, the leadership, and ethos of these approaches, the differences between them are clear and dramatic. The objectives of compliance-based programs are to prevent criminal misconduct and to reduce legal liabilities. Its leadership can be largely attorney-driven, or may come "top-down" from senior executives to lower management. Paine points out that the methods of compliance-based programs serve to reduce managerial discretion, rely on training sessions and manuals, and can function primarily through the imposition of penalties and other disincentives. Integrity-based approaches, as Paine conceives them, have as their objectives enabling responsible conduct and empowering managers' decision-making. In contrast to corporate counsel taking the lead, integrity-based programs are management driven. Thus, an integrity approach relies on leadership from management and employees, methods of education and audits, which function through the empowering of employees to make ethical decisions. It seems obvious that these approaches can lead to dramatically different organizational environments. The ethos of a compliance strategy is conformity to externally imposed standards. An integrity-based approach helps to produce a corporate culture of self-governance according to independently chosen standards, in an atmosphere more conducive of moral imagination in decision-making.

When discussing Paine's ideas with MBA students or with business leaders I often ask, "Is this just another language game?" If language structures our experience, then it is important to question concepts like these carefully, to see if they make a genuine distinction. Mission statements and codes of ethics can be more about public relations than anything else. Students especially are all too familiar with the compliance approach. They "know the drill" of ethics training, risk management seminars and online ethics quizzes. A recent example from Illinois illustrates that even academic professionals can play the game: The state mandates ethics training, followed by an exam, for all state employees. According to officials, it took most employees slightly over thirty minutes to complete the training. There was no rule about a minimum time limit. Out of thousands of employees, several took significantly less time to finish the test, leaving one bureaucrat to openly express a suspicion that cheat sheets may have been used.[11] When a professor completed the exam in barely over six minutes, state officials sent him a notice of non-compliance with the training, despite his perfect score. He was threatened with punishment, even dismissal, if he would not agree to retake it in the "proper" timeframe. The case went to court, where the professor prevailed.[12] Occasionally, someone in my classes will admit that fellow employees develop cheat sheets for those online tutorials, which is quite ironic—cheating, on an ethics quiz! So, there is a significant difference here, it is not just a matter of semantics nor a clever marketing strategy. An integrity-based program provides a qualitative difference for management's approach to ethical decision-making.

An integrity-based approach, focusing as it does on that which is internal rather than external, moves beyond the narrow limitations of legal standards to broader considerations that are not easily captured in an ethics "program" as such. The distinction is captured well by the difference between compliance and integrity. There are at least two reasons for this: First, compliance training would seem to be dedicated to the resolution of problems (legal or ethical) that are anticipated by risk management officers, not the real issues faced by management. Second, as Merton's analysis of Eichmann shows, someone with no moral imagination can painstakingly adhere to the letter of the law explicitly laid out in a compliance handbook, while knowingly but indifferently participating in unethical behaviors. "There is a moment of innocence," Merton says in *Conjectures of a Guilty Bystander*, "when action makes a great deal of sense. But who can recognize such moments? Not he who is debauched by a series of programs."[13] I believe that Merton's words hold true for organizational ethics. Only an internal, integrity-based approach to professional ethics can avoid the depths of bad faith and the logic of failure, by recognizing the importance of authenticity on behalf of management and by making room for employees to exercise freedom of moral imagination to engage in good decision-making.

Citing the examples of both Eichmann and Beech-Nut in her book, *Moral Imagination and Management Decision Making*, noted business ethicist Patricia Werhane raises the question: Which "self" do we hold responsible in cases of moral failure? It is tempting to posit a self that is independent of all roles—*that* is the self that we want to hold responsible for misdeeds. "But," Werhane retorts, "what is the nature of the non-role-defined self?"[14] If I eliminate all of the roles which I occupy, what is left? On the other hand, however, we must not commit the fallacy of identifying the self merely with the roles which one occupies—this is surely bad faith. Is the resolution of this difficulty simply a matter of improved education or better ethics training programs?

Too often these programs fail to develop or inspire empathetic understanding or creative moral deliberation. Ethics training and programs cannot be successful when they only supply the external features of decision-making. More emphasis could be placed on the internal features of moral deliberation, such as inspiring empathetic understanding and moral imagination. However, this approach requires a different strategy than appeals to moral theories; it requires recognizing the role of emotions in ethical decision-making.

Ethics and Emotions

Standard forms of ethics training make sense to us, whether they strive toward an ideal of integrity or merely attempt to ensure compliance. The training becomes part of our routine, tedious perhaps or sometimes irrelevant, but comfortable to us because it has a rational structure. There is a "method to the madness" of ethics training since it takes specific forms which are organized, cerebral, and systematic. One of the consequences of the Enlightenment shift to a focus on moral theory was the structuralizing of moral decision-making. An emphasis was placed on capturing in a theoretical paradigm the essence of deliberation and a rational foundation of values. Theories attempted to express a basic principle or principles, which serve to ground value judgments. Theories also attempted to expose the formal structure of good reasoning by developing reasoned justifications for ordinary choices. So, Jeremy Bentham attempts to express the categories of moral reasoning which he believes human beings use on a daily basis, even though they may not realize that they are doing so. Likewise, Immanuel Kant takes his theoretical paradigm to provide the basis for judging whether one's will conforms to the highest requirements of morality, the "moral law within." Nevertheless, another consequence of this Enlightenment perspective has had a more negative effect, which is the privileging of reason over emotion. Particularly when it involves moral judgments, reason is seen as objective and as establishing a standard (Bentham's "greatest good" or Kant's "moral law"), whereas the emotions are viewed as subjective, relative, and arbitrary. Consequently, traditional ethical theorists rejected the emotions as contrary to reason.

However, the result is that over time we have come to distrust moral evaluations which appeal to or arise from anything other than rational forms of consciousness, and we have lost touch with the emotions as conveyors of moral intuitions and sensitivities. Given the status of the rational account of morality in the philosophical tradition, only a few recent philosophers have investigated the significance of the emotions to our lives, especially moral judgments. One such philosopher, Robert Solomon, has drawn an explicit connection between them. Referring to our "emotional-ethical" lives, Solomon asserts that,

> emotions have meaning. They do not just "fit" into our lives but shape our lives through their conceptions and evaluations of the situations in which we find (or could find) ourselves, of the people we deal with, and of ourselves and our place in the world.[15]

This somewhat artificial separation of reason from emotions explains, I believe, part of the disconnect with ethics training that one feels, between the principles and structure of the decision-making paradigm and one's innermost moral instincts and perceptions. Let me illustrate with a true dilemma of my own, from a simple situation that anyone might encounter on a given day.

On the drive home late one night from teaching an evening class, followed by a few hours of research in a university library, I was forced by a traffic light to stop in front of a local pub. As I approached the intersection a young, intoxicated patron stumbled through its doors onto the sidewalk. Barely able to walk, he proceeded to attempt to drive his car, which he had conveniently parked directly in front of the pub, on the very street where I was waiting. He fumbled for his keys, which he dropped on several occasions; he even paused to take care of some unpleasant business. . . . I watched all of this with great curiosity and admittedly some disgust, letting the traffic light cycle through several times, since no other cars had approached the intersection. Eventually this person was able to start the car, but because he was parallel parked and given his condition, he was not able to drive away immediately. I suddenly recalled that a patrol car would often sit, late at night, in the parking lot of a quick-mart two blocks from my location. As the light turned green, I quickly drove down and, sure enough, an officer was there. I hurriedly described what I had seen and the officer sped toward the pub. I had to circle the block to come back to that location, but out of curiosity I did so, and found the officer with the inebriated offender sitting on the sidewalk and sick again. I did not wait to see if an arrest ensued, this time when the traffic light turned green I drove home. I do not know what happened to this person.

Later, I thought to myself, "Why did I do that?" Like MacIntyre's analysis of the man working in his garden, the answer is not altogether clear. From a utilitarian perspective, perhaps I was considering the "greatest good" since this person's likely incarceration pales in comparison to the damage that he could do if he were to drive in such a condition. Moreover, the greatest good for the greatest number would definitely maintain that the privacy and individual freedom of this person, intoxicated as he was, should be sacrificed for the safety and security of the community. His right to become inebriated, and then attempt to drive, is outweighed by the safety concerns of society as a whole. On the other hand, from a deontological perspective, one could consider it a duty to report such an incident; this explains the outrage and disappointment at the passersby in the Genovese case. Someone might make the argument that I was morally obligated—I had a fundamental duty, (whether to society, to God, or to the "moral law" itself), to intervene in this situation. Perhaps I considered these things as I waited at the traffic light. Perhaps I considered other things: it might be the case that unconsciously, in line with egoism, I was suppressing an incident from six years before, in which my wife was involved in an "accident" (recalling George Carlin's definition) involving a drunken driver that "totaled" our car and wrecked our finances at the time. Whenever the insurance company "totals" your car, you do not get the full price of what it would cost you to replace the vehicle, you receive the market value of the vehicle in the condition it was in prior to the catastrophic wreck. Hence, a vehicle worth $4,500 to the owner, in terms of remaining loan payments and replacement costs, may only be worth

$900 in terms of the market value of the insured car itself. You can guess what happens when one tries to replace a $4,500 vehicle with the $900 allotted by the insurance company. Perhaps the resentment of that situation, caused by an intoxicated driver years before, incited me to take retaliation against this would-be driver. In light of this history, it could be that I simply took delight in seeing someone "busted" for something that had once harmed me. So, egoism could provide a reasonable explanation as to why I acted as I did in this situation. On the other hand, maybe it was simply a case of virtue: I reported the situation to the proper authorities, simply because it was prudent and socially desirable, the "right thing to do" under the circumstances. Reporting the person to a nearby authority, strikes a convenient balance between doing nothing and directly confronting the offender (who appeared larger than I, but in his condition, I think that I could have prevailed in a scuffle!).

Occasionally, I will tell this story in class and ask students to speculate as to my motive(s). All sorts of considerations come to light: Were my family or relatives in any danger? Were they possibly out at this time of night, and potential victims of this person's poor choices? Would I be morally blameworthy if I had looked the other way, minded my own business, and proceeded home? What if the police were not close by at the quick-mart? Would it have been morally acceptable to say, "Well, I tried, I did what I was supposed to do, so I bear no responsibility for any consequences"? If the police were not two blocks away, if I had called "911" on my cell phone (what if I had no cell phone?), should I then go home in peace and guilt-free, believing that I had fulfilled all of my possible ethical duties? Did I have a *duty* to confront this person myself? What if the person drove away from the pub, instigated a violent crash, and caused the deaths of other people? Would I bear any guilt for those consequences? Should I feel guilt? Even if I did feel badly, would it be justified? Do I bear the slightest responsibility for any consequences of this person's behavior? If so, why? These are difficult questions, with no easily determined answers, and students often vigorously argue about differing viewpoints—all from a relatively simple incident encountered on my drive home. How easy it would have been to literally "look the other way" and drive on, knowing (as I did) that none of my family were threatened by this person's poor behavior. Not to forget, we have not even considered the ethical duties of persons working in the pub, who may have legal (not just moral) obligations to restrict sales of beverages to obviously intoxicated persons and to protect the public by ensuring that these patrons do not attempt to drive away from the establishment in their inebriated condition.

Moral theory can address some of these questions, particularly the ones dealing with consequences and duties. However, some of these questions are not approachable through moral theory, but seem to be more matters of moral intuitions or sensitivities. To put it another way, the variety of moral theories can provide one with various *rationales* for my action, or even justifications for condemning inaction or other alternatives. But the theories cannot explain my *desire* to act. Ethics training can supply the framework from which to analyze my motives, but doesn't begin to touch my *motivation* for acting in this situation. There is a big difference between *explaining my justifications* and motives for doing an act, and *understanding my desire*, my motivation for engaging in an action. Those questions are better addressed through a philosophical analysis of emotions, not reason, through "spiritual" lenses (for lack of a better word), not those of systems of ethics.

In *The Abuse of Casuistry*, Albert Jonsen and Stephen Toulmin articulate an anti-theoretical perspective on ethical reflection, opposing what they refer to as "the tyranny of principles."[16] The authors recount their experience as members of a national commission for the protection of human subjects of biomedical and behavioral research in the mid to late 1970s. The eleven members of the commission came from a wide variety of backgrounds; they represented an equally wide range of interests and professions. Surprisingly to the authors, although the chairperson joked about having matters of great ethical importance being decided by a six to five vote, this did not happen. On the contrary, as long as the deliberations and policy recommendations remained on a practical level there was an amazing degree of agreement. However, when members engaged in discussions or informal conversations on theoretical perspectives, the differences between them were obvious and quite dramatic. Although their outcomes and recommendations on practical issues showed great consensus, their theoretical commitments and philosophical justifications were quite different. Jonsen and Toulmin came away from this experience with the conviction that moral reasoning which begins from a concrete situation, not from a theoretical perspective or general principle, is more indicative of how human beings wrestle with and decide difficult situations. As soon as discussions turned to theoretical principles, members the commission would argue in separate directions, but staying with the concrete features of particular scenarios and then reasoning to a resolution, specific moral values emerged. Similarly with students' responses to my personal ethical dilemma: They will often reach a consensus about what I should have done in that situation, the limits of my actions and the praise- or blame-worthiness of some choices, but they rarely agree on the underlying theoretical reasons for their conclusion. What this reveals, I contend, is that we do not rely on moral theories as much as some philosophers would have us believe. Whenever we confront morally difficult situations, we may not be utilizing rational moral principles as the Enlightenment tradition suggests; we may be making use of something deeper but no less complex.

Ethics and Moral Imagination

Some people believe that the best way to resolve moral dilemmas is to clarify the ethical principles or rules governing one's profession and then learn to rationally apply them to real-life situations that we find ourselves in every day. Most ethics training programs presuppose this belief and operate in this manner. In his book, *Moral Imagination*, Mark Johnson argues that an important feature of our humanity is missing from this approach: the role of imagination in moral reasoning. "Our moral understanding depends in large measure on various structures of imagination, such as images, image schemas, metaphors, narratives, and so forth."[17] Johnson believes that moral reasoning is an imaginative activity because imagination is required to "discern what is morally relevant in situations, to understand empathetically how others experience things, and to envision the full range of possibilities open to us in a particular case."[18] Johnson uses empirical findings of cognitive science as a basis for arguing that the foundation of morality is not rational principles or systems of calculation structured in the mind, but is grounded in our bodily experience and imaginative capacity.

Although Johnson's view is innovative and "disruptive" to traditional views of morality, it may not be as radical as it is purported to be. This view has no doubt been neglected in the history of philosophy: the connection between morality and embodiment, values and emotions, morality and imagination. But it is not an altogether foreign idea. There is a hint of this notion even in Plato. A traditional approach to ethics has been to focus on Book IV of the *Republic*, in which Socrates provides an argument which posits three parts of the soul: the appetites, the spirited, and the rational. (Recall the discussion from the second chapter: According to Plato, these three parts correspond to three classes of persons that constitute a city, since the city is the "individual writ large.") The description given in Book IV of the *Republic* is often linked to Plato's allegory of a chariot in the *Phaedrus*, another of his dialogues. In that allegory the "spirited" part of the soul is compared with a chariot driver attempting to successfully navigate his rig, which is being pulled by two horses down a treacherous road. Like the characters in an old-time television Western, the white horse is good and temperate; it represents reason, of course. The dark horse is bad and unruly, representing the passions, desires, and emotions. However, this traditional interpretation is an oversimplification because it neglects the implications of arguments of Socrates in Book IX of the *Republic*. In this later chapter, Socrates provides a complex psychological theory of pleasure that is connected throughout the discussion with the *desire* to live a virtuous life. Likewise, in Book VI of the *Nicomachean Ethics*, Aristotle uses language to structure an attempt to get at the question Plato is raising in the latter book of the *Republic*, employing the notion of "reasoned desire." This concept effectively holds unified what traditional philosophy, especially after the Enlightenment, separated and distinguished: our embodied relations and interactions with the world, from our thoughts and capacity to reason. Traditional philosophy's interpretation of this bifurcation was so strong that even later philosophers like David Hume were understood as merely "taking the other side" of the issue when he argued that reason is subordinate to the emotions, an interpretation which also seems to miss a subtle but important point in his philosophy. Therefore, I believe that there is recognition of the importance of the emotions and moral imagination in the history of philosophy, but it has taken someone like Johnson and developments in cognitive science to further this approach to moral decision-making.

Indeed, we are learning much about how the mind works from empirical research in cognitive science. We are discovering how neural networks function and give rise to the capacities for consciousness, including sensory perception and language processing. These developments are challenging our conceptions of the self and self-identity. Johnson believes that as imaginative synthesizing creatures, our self-identity and moral development are linked to narrative contexts (similar to MacIntyre's concept of a "narrative self") that are imbued with metaphorical meanings and imaginative structures. The narrative self stands in stark contrast to the traditional self, split between reason and desire. By this account, we experience and learn through social situations which behaviors are acceptable or unacceptable, developing over time the ability to recognize prototypical situations and developing the capacity to discriminate or discern aspects of non-prototypical situations. On this view then, morality is based not on ingrained moral principles nor self evident truths, but rests on a narrative conception of the self in which values are gained from experiences and social contexts in which we live. This provides the basis for the claim that moral values are grounded not on reason but on our embodied experience, which would therefore include emotions, desire, and even empathy.[19] The latter emotion, empathy, has been attributed by Marc Hauser in *Moral Minds*, to the presence of networks of "mirror neurons" in the brain. "The mirror neuron system is," according to Hauser, "an important engine for simulating emotions and thoughts—for getting under someone else's skin, feeling what it is like to be another human."[20] Without reducing the whole of conscious down to brain states, it is nevertheless possible to recognize an inherent connection between our embodied, emotional existence, and our moral sensitivities. As Hauser notes,

> We have some sense of what it might feel like to be another living creature. We can imagine what it is like to walk in their shoes. Empathy is a fundamental link in our ethical behavior.[21]

The works of Hauser, Solomon, and Johnson are important because they place our reasoning about ethical issues on, if not a different basis, at least a different level. By their lights, ethical reflection is an expression of our embodiment and a manifestation of our desires and goals, as well as our emotional ties; it is not so much about the rational application of general principles to particular situations. From this perspective, enhancing moral sensitivity is not so much about inculcating recognition of higher rational principles in the minds of persons, but involves nurturing moral imagination. Like developing the ability to appreciate a piece of music or poetry, enriching moral sensitivity is a matter of both critical reflection and creativity.

There are at least three aspects of moral imagination that are important and applicable to fostering critical reflection on issues of professional ethics: first, the power to recognize the dominant linguistic schemas, particularly metaphors, which structure our experience; second, an ability to envision alternatives and creative possibilities in response to ethical dilemmas; and third, a heightened capacity to empathize with others, to identify one's self with others. I believe that each one of these features can be found in the life and work of Merton, and as I discuss each one briefly, I will attempt to make that connection.

Both Mark Johnson's and Eric Mount's focus on metaphors and narratives is further evidence that language matters. First, realizing how words (which have values embedded in them) are brought together to form conceptual schemas underscores the power that language has to structure our thinking, our beliefs, and our self-understanding as human beings. Moral imagination empowers one to recognize linguistic structures that shape experience. It provides a person with the capacity to unpack the dominant metaphors that are shaping their ideas about the world and interactions with other people; this is one of its greatest strengths. For example, Johnson supports his argument by citing a passage from Merton's *Love and Living* (though Merton is not listed in his index) in which Merton describes the "package concept of love."[22] Johnson uses the insights of Merton to analyze the metaphorical aspects of personal narratives; in this case, a prostitute's grappling with self-understanding through telling a story about her first encounter, how she began to turn tricks. Johnson sees the metaphorical model of "sex is a market transaction . . . love as a market transaction" as part of the woman's socio-psychological conditioning. "Though he doesn't call it metaphoric," Johnson states, "Thomas Merton has analyzed the nature of this metaphorical framework, its pervasiveness in our society, and the ways in which it undermines the possibility of genuine love."[23] Merton's notion of the package concept of love serves as a point of interpretation for Johnson's analysis of the woman's description of love as a market transaction. The clarity and power of Merton's moral imagination is evident in his "unpacking" and exposure of a conceptual schema of capitalism applied to our personal lives. Of course, we become conditioned to view things this way, not only concerning sexual relations but with our entire self-identities. Students especially speak about "marketing yourself," or the necessity to "sell yourself" when applying for a job. Using a metaphor of Adam Smith from the capitalistic economic foundation which structures so much of our experience, all of life becomes a "marketplace," including ideas, values, even love. However, the use of moral imagination provides one with the ability to recognize dominant metaphors and concepts that frame our thoughts and values.

There are numerous other examples that one could provide from the variety of professions. These metaphors, phrases and linguistic schemas often betray our best motives, especially in the workplace. Good intentions alone, as Laura Nash points out, are not enough to assure moral outcomes. She inquires,

> Why do failures of conscience occur in business? When a company begins with a strategic goal of providing a customer-oriented product or service of quality, why does it end up creating a mediocre, unresponsive product and engaging in unfair, deceptive and potentially injurious activities?[24]

The answer has to do with the gap between beliefs and actions, between motives and implementations. Sometimes the best decisions, the most ethically sound institutional policies, are implemented in ways that are contrary to the values they were designed to uphold. A good example, which we often discuss in bioethics classes, is the concept of "informed consent." In Socratic fashion, we could analyze informed consent by breaking it down into its components. In a medical context, to be "informed" obviously means being adequately advised about treatment options, potential consequences, and costs. Moreover, "consent" indicates properly agreeing to a recommended course of treatment. Interestingly, informed consent is not part of the Hippocratic tradition, and in the centuries-long history of caring for the health of human beings, the notion of informed consent has only emerged in the last fifty years. In fact, only since the 1980s has the concept of informed consent gained prominence. Prior to that time, the paradigm for a physician's relationship to patients was echoed in the title of a popular television show of that period, "Father Knows Best." Different explanations could be offered for this shift in medical ethics. An idealist might say that an expanding notion of human dignity and patient's rights was the primary motivating factor. An empiricist might say that expanding technologies and treatment options necessitated a new approach to interactions between doctors and their patients. Regardless of the causes, the concept of informed consent has generated new responsibilities for relating to patients and new institutional policies to safeguard the values of rights and respect. If competent persons are not fully informed, then they cannot be fully actualizing their freedom, rights or responsibilities since some options have been withheld from them. If they merely acquiesce to family or physician pressures, then again they are not genuinely exercising their personal freedom in a way that honors the dignity of being human and respects the rights of each individual.

Over time, however, something interesting has happened to this important concept, particularly in the way that it is assumed to be protected. Historically speaking, first came discussions with one's physician, accompanied by a patient's acquiescence, perhaps noted in a patient's chart, but little else. Next came a one-page form, to be filled out and signed by the patient, acknowledging consultation with the physician but often before even having met with the doctor. Nowadays, in many locations informed consent is handled electronically, as paragraph after paragraph of legalese scrolls down a small screen about the size of a credit card reader, in barely legible font, endorsed with the click of a button. It makes no small difference, for at a time when medical technology has increased exponentially, the once touted value of informed consent, based as it is on the dignity and rights of every human being, has become a trivial ritual serving as a *precondition to receiving treatment* rather than a recognition of the communication of options prior to selecting a type or level of care that one desires. Moreover, it is fascinating to ponder that what began as a gesture to protect the inherent worth of human beings morphed over time into a procedural ritual designed to protect institutions. Nurses, in the end, bear much of the burden of either communicating relevant information or of attempting to construct better lines of communication between patients, patients' families, and physicians. As a result, they are placed in many difficult ethical dilemmas that pit their professional role as members of a hospital or healthcare organization against their traditional role as patient advocates.

This is one example, among many, of the way in which concepts and metaphors structure our lives, and how the application of Merton's call for a critical "Socratism" can reveal the moral nuances of linguistic structures. Moreover, this example also exposes how concerns of risk management and legal counsel can trump the actual ethical dilemmas that people "in the trenches" encounter on a daily basis; a confirmation of Paine's argument. Contemplation and moral imagination can provide the means by which we envision better procedures, (in this case, more patient-centered) policies, and supportive environments that healthcare professionals can trust to voice their concerns about patient issues. It is not surprising that many ethical dilemmas, particularly in a hospital setting, occur because of poor communication between professionals and patients. The issue of informed consent merely represents one way that contemplation can empower moral imagination to reconceptualize the linguistic structures that govern our professional lives, and to provide the basis for genuine leadership in adequately addressing fundamental moral issues that are pivotal to the exercise of professional ethics.

Second, moral imagination also empowers one to conceive of alternatives in moral dilemmas, possibilities and options that theoretical preferences and procedural rule-following might not be able to conceptualize. Contemplation provides one with moral imagination to conceive of creative resolutions to difficult choices, ways of seeing the problem and possibilities for approaching it from new directions. This feature of moral imagination is especially needed in contexts in which decision-making becomes a matter of routine, merely following institutional procedures or adhering to a professional code. That kind of decision-making is false from the start because it attempts to plot individual and often unique cases along prototypical lines. It can be difficult to detect ethical conflicts or even the presence of moral issues in environments which rely on a decision-making strategy of adherence to organizational policies; this virtually ensures the structure of a "logic of failure." Moreover, it is difficult to take responsible action in unique or pressing situations whenever one lacks an ability to assess options and imagine alternatives. I believe that many of the young professionals in Fischman's research (discussed in Chapter Three) become disillusioned or "burnout" because they feel trapped and alienated in environments that do not permit the exercise of moral freedom and do not encourage moral imagination. In the absence of freedom and creativity, human beings lose a sense of purpose. Moral imagination empowers one to rediscover purpose in what they do.

Merton's point about the "forced systematization of life" is indicative of the experience that professionals often have of getting lost in the system. Through the tempo of work, the formation and standardization of work patterns, the routines of professional life can have the effect of blinding one from the larger purpose for which they exist. The necessity of watching every step, the pressure of following every minute detail of bureaucratic mandates (and the documentation of them!), adhering to every ideological protocol can cause professionals to focus on details of the present moment and forget the primary purpose for their actions. Like the proverbial wanderer who is so focused on moving from one tree to the next, the "forced systematization of life" can take away our sense of the forest. "Lost" becomes a major metaphor which expresses how professionals feel at these points in their work lives. The moral imagination that one can exercise in contemplation can restore a sense of purpose and help one to regain the satisfaction that comes from being part of a profession. As mentioned earlier, it is a characteristic of professions that they are intended to serve others, but when we lose sight of that feature, whenever we feel like we are serving organizational bureaucracy rather than the well-being of others, this can lead to alienation and frustration. It can take the joy and self-actualization away from work, even robbing one of the gratification of a job well done. The noise of everyday life can drown out the harmony of professions seeking to serve others. Moral imagination restores one's ability to see opportunities for aligning motives and rediscovering the larger purposes that first attracted one to a profession. The self-knowledge gained through contemplation can direct and re-inspire one to desire achievement of excellence, and it can restore one's capacity for compassion.

A third reason that moral imagination empowers ethical decision-making is even more directly related to Merton. Moral imagination strengthens our capacity for empathy. As Mark Johnson and others have pointed out, traditional moral theories have almost completely neglected this aspect of our humanity. Earlier, I mentioned that both Plato and Aristotle have positive references to the emotions that have been skewed or misinterpreted in the philosophical tradition. The same could be said for other philosophical treatments which followed; that is, until we reach a period known as the Scottish Enlightenment. An excellent treatment of the emotions, particularly empathy, is given by Adam Smith in his *Theory of Moral Sentiments*. Though more widely known for his groundbreaking *Wealth of Nations*, his earlier work on the sentiments actually lays much of the foundation for concepts that go unjustified in the latter work. This sets up the "Adam Smith problem," the issue of reconciling Smith's earlier view which seems to insightfully describe human empathy and the importance of it for human well-being, with his later view in *Wealth of Nations* which appears to advocate egoism, selfishness, and individualism. James Otteson has recently shown that it is possible to reconcile these two works and resolve the problem, which provides even more justification for unpacking powerful capitalistic metaphors which structure our lives.[25]

Another philosopher who was part of the Scottish Enlightenment was eighteenth-century philosopher David Hume. Hume argued against the rationalists, who believed that ethical values were either innate or self-evident, for an empirical understanding of ethics as really a matter of emotion. Citing the work of Annette Baier in challenging the traditional interpretation of Hume's moral theory, Johnson argues that, "Hume's sentiment for the welfare of others is a blending of feeling, imagination, and reason."[26] For Johnson, the key to empathetic imagination is to imagine ourselves in the place of another person.

> Unless we can put ourselves in the place of another, unless we can enlarge our own perspective through an imaginative encounter with the experience of others, unless we can't let our own values and ideals be called into question from various points of view, we cannot be morally sensitive.[27]

This implies that moral imagination is shared. Echoing the research findings of Hauser, according to Johnson, moral imagination is just as public as other social relations which people form. "Imagination as I have described it," Johnson boldly claims, "is the primary means by which social relations are constituted."[28] Taking up the position of another person, visualizing one's self in different circumstances, requires an act of imaginative experience and contemplative reflection. Johnson's argument also allows us to see Kant's moral philosophy in a slightly different light. The principle of universalizability which he advocates only makes sense in the context of an ability to visualize oneself in the position of another. Kant's deontological theory admonishes one to ensure one's will is acting in conformity with the moral law by employing the "categorical imperative." (Kant says there is one and only one categorical imperative, but then proceeds to offer different formulations of it; the reason Nietzsche says of Kant, he takes common sense and states it in a way that the person with common sense can't understand it anymore!) A commonsense way of stating the categorical imperative, to "act only on the maxim you could will, at the same time, to be a universal law," is nothing other than the Golden Rule, to "do unto others as you would have them do unto you." It is clear that more than reason is necessary for the implementation of the categorical imperative, for it is not possible to actualize this process in a purely cerebral manner. Kant's view only makes sense when it recognizes and incorporates moral imagination. Discerning that which is universalizable, grasping the existential import of treating others the way you would like to be treated, can only be fully realized and effective through the use of moral imagination.

It is also clear from the work of Hauser, Solomon, Johnson, and a growing number of others, that moral imagination requires contemplation. Moral theories may broaden one's understanding of factors in a dilemma, but they do not determine the depth of that understanding because the theories themselves cannot inspire moral imagination. Rather, they presuppose it. Contemplation allows time and silence, a quiet time of solitude for the moral imagination to develop and mature. The exercise of moral imagination requires time for critical reflection. The effort spent in contemplation is rewarded by an enrichment of one's discernment and depth of understanding. By situating moral values in the context of our emotions, as these authors have done, we recover a sense of the source of Merton's insightfulness and his ability to conceive of alternatives on moral issues (particularly those of politics, race, and religion). Merton's contemplative insights were not the result of a flight of reason away from the world, but the empathetic and purposeful turning of spirit toward the world. Contemplative reflection allowed Merton to develop power of moral imagination to envision better ways for us to relate to each other, working with and serving one another. So, beyond the topics of politics, religion, and so forth, I believe that a Mertonesque insightfulness and application of moral imagination to issues in professional ethics can reinvigorate and transform our working lives. Professional ethics, to be fully realized, demands greater attention not to moral theorizing but to increasing our capacities of moral imagination.

CHAPTER FIVE

MORAL IMAGINATION AND LEADERSHIP

Merton's call to contemplation is a call neither to enlightened self-interest nor to otherworldly detachment. Rather, Merton's invitation to contemplative practice views contemplation as an extended call to action. He calls us to a journey of self-examination and application in the concrete situations of everyday life, to improve our individual and social lives. As the work of Mount, Schmidt, and others has shown, we need a transformation of work, not merely on the individual level but also on the corporate level; it does little good to reinvigorate one person's attitude or values unless there can also be a rejuvenation of the institutional context which that person occupies. This kind of change cannot come from shallow self-help programs and it cannot come through disengagement; these often lead to pessimism and cynicism that only promote deeper role-playing and greater organizational hegemony. I have argued that Merton's contemplative approach can lead to a revision of professional ethics through its connection with moral imagination. But moving beyond this individual level to the organizational structures of professional life will demand much more. The journey of critical reflection and its application involve self-discipline to be sure; yet, it additionally calls for leadership. Using moral imagination to transcend the divisions between private and professional morality and to transform the organizations that structure our professional lives will require leadership. Such changes will have need of leadership that is transformative, but not necessarily heroic.

Leadership programs, research, and books are plentiful. I would venture a guess that, second only to books about Lincoln, leadership is one of the most written about topics (and of course, some books discuss both Lincoln and leadership, since his life provides such excellent examples and principles). These sources highlight various aspects, components, and characteristics of leadership. At best, some theories help define and identify traits of leadership and instill a sense of direction in obtaining them. At worst, these resources become instruction manuals on how to feign leadership, essentially allowing one to fake it for as long as possible—either because one simply aspires to it or because one has been placed (perhaps unwittingly) in a position of responsibility which requires it. This latter kind of leadership is unquestionably bad faith, but it happens quite often in business, sometimes unintentionally: the top sales producer or most efficient project member gets promoted into a leadership position, where they are suddenly no longer directly involved in sales or project development but are now thrust into a management position, often unprepared and sometimes against their own desires.

With all of these resources, there are naturally many different theories of leadership. As we have discussed, leadership is important to transforming professions in ways that would incorporate the insights from Merton's life and writings. However, examination of a broad spectrum of leadership theories would go too far astray from the purposes of this study. It is useful though to examine two popular but widely divergent theories, Bernard Bass's theory of "transformative leadership" and Joseph Badaracco's concept of "quiet leadership," to see how these two drastically different theories might yield some common themes of leadership that might change the nature of professional ethics in a positive manner.

Transformative Leadership

For decades, Bernard Bass has been one of the foremost researchers of leadership. He has authored numerous books and over 60 journal articles on the subject.[1] In collaboration with other researchers, Bass has investigated many aspects of leadership. He has joined with many scholars in studying characteristics of persons recognized as effective leaders, whether or not those leaders were deemed morally good (since villains may also be efficient leaders). The result of his research and collaboration has culminated in the concept of "transformative leadership." Bass distinguishes between two types of leadership: transactional and transformative. Both types have an ethical ingredient. Transactional leadership is *contractual*; it functions along the lines of social contract theory, by compliance with leadership's demands and impersonal application of approved standards. Transformative leadership is more *covenantal* and community oriented, functioning through inspirational motivation and personal consideration. Though some critics have charged that transformative leadership overlooks ethical concerns, Bernard Bass and Paul Steidlmeier persuasively argue that authentic leadership must recognize traditional ethical principles.[2] Moreover, in order to be genuine, these principles must be evident in the character of the leader. In other words, the authority of the leader can often be based on that person's moral credibility. If others observe that a leader behaves amorally or is indifferent to ethical concerns, or if a leader is interpreted as acting primarily on the basis of self-interest, in either case the leader loses credibility.

It would be a fair guess that a mix of personal and institutional interests motivate most managers and leaders. In the worst of circumstances, leadership mired in bad faith is authoritarian, myopic, and rule utilitarian. Authentic leadership, which is the only sort of leadership that will have the moral power to transform the disconnectedness and contradictions of professional life, must avoid the two extremes of passive indifference on one side and bad faith on the other side. To acquiesce to institutional demands, organizational structures or professional codes is not genuine leadership. "Laissez faire leaders avoid leading," claim Bass and Steidlmeier in their study of ethics and leadership.[3] Such a position is not authentic leadership management, but an oxymoron, a contradiction, precisely because it fails to lead at all. There is no opportunity for insight or moral transformation in this case because of a denial that any problem exists: "Follow the rules, adhere to the code, and you'll be fine." On the other hand, leadership exhibits bad faith when moral values are not a priority but are jettisoned in favor of expediency and self-gain. There is a kind of leadership that is alluring and enthusiastic. It can be successful at motivating people and achieving particular goals, but its leadership is manipulative and deceptive, exploiting and alienating associates and subordinates.

According to Bass and Steidlmeier, there are three ethical components of authentic leadership. First is the moral character of the leader. Second is the perceived legitimacy of the ethical values exhibited by the leader's actions, values which are accepted or rejected by subordinates. Third is the morality of the actions, choices, and procedures which subordinates and leaders engage in collectively. Implicit in their argument is a high-level of moral maturity and ethical reasoning on the part of authentic leaders. These components are exhibited, as we have seen, in the context of institutions and organizational structures which can complicate moral decision-making and right actions. Thus, subordinates give attention not only to the moral content of decisions but also to the processes by which interaction with leadership takes place.

Of course, most leaders would show some mix of both transactional and transformative styles, though it is likely that one's type of leadership exhibits one style most of the time. Rather than relying on coercion or social pressure, Bass and Steidlmeier argue that transformational leadership recognizes the freedom of persons and seeks to motivate through persuasion and the development of moral imagination. Leadership that operates in bad faith acts contrary to these concerns. Hence, what separates bad-faith leaders from authentic leaders is the moral foundation that underlies their thoughts, actions, and approaches to ethical dilemmas. Authentic transformational leadership eschews radical egoism (manipulation being a characteristic of leadership in bad faith) because it refuses to acknowledge human freedom. Authentic leadership recognizes the importance of a unity of the self with others, it acknowledges the autonomy and dignity of each person, and it respects the intellectual development of every individual.

Quiet Leadership

Harvard Business School professor Joseph Badaracco advocates what he calls "quiet leadership." In contrast to the heroic type of leadership, in which a person undertakes a dramatic action and fights aggressively to overcome a tremendous problem, quiet leadership involves more subtle, practical, yet responsible ways of resolving ordinary ethical issues that commonly occur in professional life. Passive indifference, we have seen, is not acceptable, but too much boldness can lead to catastrophe. Reason must be able to lead us to some middle ground, following Aristotle, between these two extremes. Recognizing that "it is hard to do a great thing suddenly," Badaracco's conception of quiet leadership does not try to change an entire system or redirect the whole organization in one day; however, it does not accept excuses for doing nothing (even though some of the strategies he suggests might be interpreted that way). Rather, quiet leadership attempts to manage difficult ethical situations through small, almost insignificant actions which ultimately make a difference. "Quiet leadership," says Badaracco, "is an act of faith: an expression of confidence in the ultimate force of what [Albert] Schweitzer called 'small and obscure deeds.'"[4] Using examples from business and management, he tries to show how persons can attempt to bridge that gap between private and professional morality, living by their values and satisfying professional responsibilities but without jeopardizing one's reputation or career.

Badaracco's notion of quiet leadership has much to recommend, but aspects of it can be misinterpreted or appropriated in malevolent fashion. It highlights the difficulties of making decisions in complex situations, with limited information and often little cooperation from others, and it differs dramatically from traditional models and narratives of leadership. A heroic form of leadership, the popular view, stresses the importance of purity of motives, but Badaracco suggests that one should trust mixed motives as a recognition of the complexity of both the outside world and our inner selves. Recalling the title of a book by Nietzsche, Badaracco suggests that we should acknowledge that leader's motives are almost always, "human, all too human." He contends that quiet leaders are successful because of a mixture of self-interested and altruistic motives—not despite them. However, Badaracco has to assume throughout his description of this concept that ethical behavior, doing the right thing, is the starting point for one's deliberations and actions. Interpreted in this charitable light, his recommendation is not only rooted in a realistic conception of human nature but it also manifests a desire for authenticity. Interpreted in a negative way, these recommendations become justification for laziness and self-interest. Badaracco goes to great lengths to ensure that the former interpretation is recognized as a characteristic of quiet leadership. He insists that unraveling motives and discerning character is like trying to unravel a spider's web. So, if we want to "really understand why people do what they do, we have to get our heads out of the clouds, be realistic, and see others and ourselves as we really are."[5] Badaracco's realism notwithstanding, I am suggesting that getting one's head out of the clouds, seeing others and ourselves as we are, requires a Mertonesque commitment to critical self-reflection and contemplation. Without meditation and devotion to a spiritual process of seeing the big picture, one risks the danger of getting lost in a fog of the complexities of motives and outcomes.

Quiet leadership may also involve a willingness to bend the rules, according to Badaracco. There is a great scene from the movie *Pirates of the Caribbean* in which the daughter of the governor of the island, kidnapped by pirates, appeals to the rules of "Morgan and Bartholomew, the Order of the Brethren," the pirates' code of ethics. In an attempt to foil their plan, she demands and is granted "parley" with the pirate's leader, Captain Barbosa. Refusing her attempts to bargain, he clarifies, "you must be a pirate for the pirates' code to apply, and you are not," then he continues wryly that, moreover, "the code is more what you'd call 'guidelines' than actual rules."[6] I suspect this is the attitude that many professionals have toward their organizations' codes of ethics, and it is the perspective which many employees have of their institution's ethical pronouncements. What if breaking the rules, however, seems to be the right thing to do in a situation? What do you do? Like the scene from this movie, there are times when mechanical devotion to rules is contrary to one's goals and might even cause harm to oneself or others. While insisting that one must take the rules seriously, Badaracco suggests that there are times when moral imagination is needed to find possibilities which honor the spirit though not the letter of the law. Simply following the rules can sometimes be a way of avoiding responsibility, whereas moral imagination searches for creative ways to resolve complex ethical conflicts. Nevertheless, Badaracco struggles to distinguish bending the rules from breaking them. He attempts to disassociate quiet leadership from a disregard for the rules, instead choosing to associate this leadership with "cleverness." He acknowledges that we often associate this word with dubious characters but insists that quiet leaders do not attempt to avoid responsibility; rather, in ethically complex situations they seek ways to bend the rules in order to find practical means of meeting diverse responsibilities.

Badaracco argues, contrary to moral theorizing, that good leaders accept the value of ethical principles but do not find them useful in most situations, because individual cases are seldom clear-cut and reducible to the application of a single principle. "Quiet leaders" adopt a different attitude toward compromise, viewing these situations as opportunities to learn and develop practical wisdom. He illustrates this point with the story of a public health official in a large city, assigned by the mayor to develop a policy response to the problem of infants born to drug addicted mothers.[7] The mayor wanted to take a "get tough" approach while healthcare professionals were unwilling to turn in their patients for fear of undermining trust and rapport with patients. Through extensive negotiations, the public health official was able to approach various stakeholders in this situation, persuade them to look beyond yes/no and black/white perspectives and to think creatively about options that would satisfy all parties. The mayor, law enforcement, and public prosecutors office believed the hard-handed approach was best. Healthcare professionals and local hospitals adamantly disagreed with this strategy but acknowledged that something needed to be done. Citizens were demanding action, angry over widely publicized infant deaths and children born with severe birth defects yet without insurance coverage. By visualizing the problem in a new light, using moral imagination to explore alternatives and view options, the public health official was able to create a consensus that responded to the problem in a way that met the concerns of all parties and dealt effectively with a difficult crisis. Tough ethical choices in complex situations seldom are worked out in an imaginative way through the application of a single ethical principle. Finding creative resolutions in difficult situations is possible when one has a greater capacity for moral imagination.

Features of Authentic Leadership

Though quite different, both of these theories, transformational and quiet leadership, hold that leadership can only be authentic and effective by avoiding the extremes of passive indifference and bad faith. Examining the life and words of Thomas Merton can enhance the value and usefulness of concepts implicit in quiet and transformative leadership because his life and writings exemplify both character and wisdom.

Leadership has not only external characteristics, but internal, what was once identified as *character*. Given the importance of language in structuring our experience, it is interesting to note that this is not a word used often in our time. We are much more comfortable saying that someone "is a character," than to say that someone has character; the same can also be said of wisdom because it is rare to hear someone say "so-and-so is wise," for we simply lack a shared standard of meaning that would make these words useful. James Davidson Hunter has written the postmortem of character, pronouncing it dead in the twenty-first century and eulogizing its authority and virtue. Hunter argues that the most basic component of character is moral discipline.[8] He blames the death of character on "two toxic elements" of the twentieth century: progressivism and postmodernism; the former connected with attempts to rein in social inequalities and curb corporate power, the latter associated with the view, discussed above, that language does not have fixed meanings, only usage. Various religious and social movements attempted to revive the patient, but to no avail. With the passing of character, moral discipline passes away. However, James Q. Wilson has argued that character's demise has been greatly exaggerated. Wilson contends that there are in, human nature, elements of a natural moral sense.[9] The road to recovery of character, assuming its near-death illness, is by regaining the strength of moral discipline through its exercise. Habituation toward goodness can be done, but it must be done with integrity in mind, not mere compliance. Character is thus internal and related to self-knowledge. Merton would opt for the latter view of Wilson, I believe, because it is more consistent with his view of our humanity and is more conducive to the forces of love and hope. Moral discipline is central to the kind of leadership needed to transform the challenges of professional morality, and to renew love for and hope in the promises of professional life to make work good.

Genuine leadership is also marked by *wisdom*. Wisdom is external and recognized by others. Similar to the concept of character, however, this is not a term that one often hears. John Kekes has pointed out that, although "philosophy" by definition is supposed to be a love of wisdom, contemporary philosophy gives almost no attention to it (a possible reason that when people are searching for it, they turn to religious, mystic, or self-help sources). According to Kekes,

> Wisdom may be identified with good judgment about the evaluation of complex situations and conceptions of a good life in the light of a reflective understanding of the human condition."[10]

Unlike the wisdom of Socrates, who was attributed with wisdom for recognizing that he did not "know" some things with certainty, nor did he claim to know them, Kekes's view of wisdom is more positive, acknowledging core human values and the importance of being self-directed toward them. On the other hand, unlike "wisdom" for Aristotle, Kekes's perspective is much more than simple "prudence" because it is more than knowledge of reasonable means to achieve ends. Wisdom, for Kekes, is about *knowledge* of moral ideals and a *desire* to attain them. Furthermore, it is "action-guiding" because it "identifies both the ideals to which we may reasonably commit ourselves in pursuit of good lives and ideals incompatible with them."[11] In light of Kekes's description of wisdom, it is perhaps no surprise that psychologists, not philosophers, most recently have taken greater interest in investigating wisdom.[12]

Though various accounts give many characteristics and qualities of wisdom, I want to focus on three common ones which are evident in the life and work of Merton: self-knowledge, an ability to "see the big picture," and having a unity of purpose. Each one of these concepts is laced with metaphors, but they can be clarified with greater description and connection with Merton. First, self-knowledge provides one with an inner cogency that is manifested through knowing one's strengths and weaknesses, without faking it or acting in bad faith. Second, grasping the "big picture" is akin to knowing where one is on the map, recognizing what is and is not important in difficult situations, without falling prey to endemic practices of the logic of failure. Third, unity of purpose involves an ability to keep one's focus on the ultimate objectives, to have a "purity of heart" in Kierkegaard's words, without allowing the self to be reduced to a disconnected series of role-playing. These three central features of leadership emerge from the moral perspective that Merton exemplifies in *Conjectures of a Guilty Bystander*. In contrast to Wilson's lament at the loss of character in today's culture, Merton's insistence on the importance of contemplation provides the context for recognizing his contribution to the recovery and development of moral discipline. However, beyond a stark, rule-following utilitarian notion of "discipline," Merton's contemplative perspective provides moral imagination from which to understand one's self and the world in which one lives, to challenge the plurality of intentions in the world and call persons to recognize a unity of purpose that binds all of humanity.

Merton clearly links his conception of self-knowledge to the Socratic tradition, the historical Socrates of Plato's *Apology* whose mantra is "Know thyself." Socrates allegedly borrows this mantra from an engraving above the Oracle of Delphi, a temple where people came in search of divine advice and wisdom about life's most complicated problems. The story is told of a king who visited the Oracle because he envied an adjacent kingdom, and he consulted the advice of the Oracle on whether to attack it or not. The Oracle is said to have replied that, if the king should attack, "a great kingdom will fall." Thinking only of his desire for the adjacent territory, the king attacked—and as you might guess, he was soundly defeated. Why? Because he did not recognize, within himself, that he already possessed a great kingdom. Self-knowledge was, and arguably still remains, the key to interpreting the word and will of the divine spirit. This king lacked the wisdom and contemplation that would have given him strength to overcome weaknesses of will and of character.

Genuine self-knowledge is important because it gives one a clear assessment of one's strengths and weaknesses. It fulfills a desire for structure and order in one's personal, internal life. It provides the basis for genuinely productive action, which Merton characterizes as "reasoned moral action."[13] Theories of ethics, particularly Aristotle's and Kant's, object to the notion that a person can be morally lucky; that is, they reject the idea that a person can be authentically good without having first developed the *intention* to do so. Thus, self-reflection is a necessary component of living a truly moral life. As such, self-knowledge can serve as an antidote to the symptoms of an "overstimulated society" because it empowers one with discernment. It also helps one to avoid the depths of bad faith and inauthenticity, since dialectic emphasizes the importance of openness and honesty with one's self.

Merton shows how authentic leadership is not merely a display of external behaviors but is grounded in internal qualities associated with character and wisdom. Both of these, according to Merton, are developed through self-knowledge. It comes through the dialectical process, a Socratic questioning of one's self. Another insight, which Merton acquires from his experience of leading the novices, is that some of them fail in their religious quest because they give up questioning and searching. He calls this, "the worst temptation" that one could succumb to.[14] It is easy to see how one can fall prey to this temptation, however. We become so conditioned by the demands of professional life to focus on productivity and efficiency that we become increasingly pragmatic. Self-knowledge comes to be seen as a luxury, or worse, superfluous. Indeed, it is not an easy task, and Merton warns about the difficulty of overcoming inertia and delusion. However, in agreement with Socrates, it is clear that Merton believed that self-knowledge is fundamental to a truly fulfilling life, a life of character and wisdom.

Another quality of leadership that I believe is revealed in Merton's contemplative analysis is an ability to "see the big picture." Perhaps metaphysically similar to Peter Singer's concept of the "point of view of the universe," seeing the big picture is about recognizing one's place on the map. It is related to the notion discussed earlier of having a moral compass. In the disarray of confusing situations, conflicting voices, and competing values, it is important to know where one stands and to have a sense of direction. Merton describes this, occasionally, as being able to grasp things in their entirety, in their wholeness. Several examples from Merton's life illustrate this point. The most obvious one is his epiphany on a street corner in downtown Louisville, the account of which is given in *Conjectures of a Guilty Bystander*. He describes in poignant language an overwhelming experience of unity and love for others. "It was like waking from a dream of separateness," Merton says, "the whole illusion of a separate holy existence is a dream."[15] Waking up from this dream, recognizing the illusion, did not, however, cause Merton to call his vocation into question. On the contrary, it gave him a deeper sense of self-understanding and of his purpose. Merton reflects on the meaning of this experience,

> This changes nothing in the sense and value of my solitude, for it is in fact the function of solitude to make one realize such things with a clarity that would be impossible to anyone completely immersed in the other cares, the other illusions, and all the automatisms of a tightly collective existence.[16]

Finding himself and others and seeing others in himself, Merton was able to grasp his place in the universe, his reason for being.

Merton's assertion that people "completely immersed in other cares" can become trapped by "automatisms of a tightly collective existence" is highly suggestive of a concept from business ethics often used to explain moral failure in organizations, "groupthink." Groupthink is a popular concept in business management, it connotes the cohesive bond of people working closely together to support one another's beliefs and perceptions while rejecting new or unsettling outside information. In the book *Ethics and Organizational Decision Making*, Ronald Sims claims, "given the heavy emphasis on teamwork within modern organization and on groups in general, the dissemination of the groupthink concept is desperately needed and can assist us in acquiring a better understanding of why unethical behavior occurs in organizations."[17] Individual members have confidence in the group's decisions and close themselves off from alternative points of view. The result can be decisions and actions which are misinformed, unethical, and even illegal. Although it is more popular and dramatic to single out one person as responsible when the "logic of failure" inevitably happens, the truth is that it is seldom the responsibility of one individual acting in isolation. Groupthink contributes to the logic of failure because people lack the vision to see creative alternatives to situations or they lack the courage to challenge the thinking of the group. Moral imagination is an important antidote for groupthink; it mitigates against the suspension of one's critical thinking skills and it provides confidence in proposing new or innovative approaches to resolving issues. There is a popular phrase which touts the ability to "think outside the box." I am not that fond of this notion because, frankly, not enough people inside the box are thinking seriously. However, groupthink is a powerful contributor to market and moral failures, and daily news is replete with such stories that inevitably become fodder for applied ethics textbooks. The propensity of groupthink persists because constructive criticisms and innovative alternatives to ethical dilemmas are not available when persons lack moral imagination. Moreover, it is difficult to offer constructive criticisms of competing viewpoints if one does not have the capacity to visualize alternatives.

In his biography, *Thomas Merton and the Monastic Vision*, Lawrence Cunningham provides an example of groupthink which demonstrates insightful leadership qualities Merton possessed from solitude.[18] In his 1964 publication, *Seeds of Destruction*, Merton gave a penetrating critique of race relations in the United States, even warning of an impending crisis and of the need for a transformation of existing social relations. His words were not met with enthusiasm, however, and he was chided for being too pessimistic. Other Christian writers and activists, including prominent professor of American religious history, Martin Marty, pointed to the tremendous progress and promise of the Civil Rights Act just passed by Congress, guaranteeing certain rights to all persons regardless of race and outlawing forms of discrimination. But Merton saw this legislation not as the end of the movement but as its very beginning. Cunningham notes that Merton correctly perceived that the reaction to this legislation would be social upheaval, resistance, and violence.[19] Years later, Martin Marty acknowledged Merton's perceptiveness and the irony that a reclusive monk had shown more prophetic insight than others had who were more directly engaged in the events of the time.

A third feature of leadership involves recognition of and commitment to an ultimate purpose. In the movie *City Slickers*, actor Billy Crystal plays a man in mid-life crisis, who seeks relief by vacationing with two friends at a "dude ranch" and participating in a two-week cattle drive.[20] They meet the frighteningly rough and reclusive head cowboy played by Jack Palance. Chasing a stray cow, Crystal and Palance become separated from the rest of the drive and they begin to open up to one another. The urban, cubicle-dwelling Crystal finds himself alone with, but warming up to, the mysterious cowboy. Palance suggests that "city slickers" like Crystal all come to the ranch about the same time in their lives, late thirties, letting fifty weeks of stress per year put "knots in their rope" but then expecting two weeks in wide-open western atmosphere to get out all of the kinks. Away from the others, discussing life and love, Crystal even remarks to Palance, "You know what's great . . . your life makes sense to you." Palance mocks how city folk worry about "a lot of stuff that doesn't really matter," and pauses to pose the fundamental question of existence to Crystal: "Do you know what the secret of life is?" he asks, pointing upward only with his index finger. "No, what? Your finger?" replies Crystal, weakly holding up his own finger in an attempt to emulate the confident cowboy. "One thing, just one thing, You stick to that . . ." Palance asserts, but without elaborating. His curiosity piqued, Crystal asks the obvious, "What's the one thing?" Turning his finger to point directly at Crystal, Palance replies, "That's what you have to figure out." This scene is reminiscent of Søren Kierkegaard's short but penetrating book, *Purity of Heart Is to Will One Thing*. Recalling the beatitude of Jesus from the Sermon on the Mount, that the pure in heart shall see God, Kierkegaard argues that purity of heart involves a turning away from self-deception and bad faith.[21] Kierkegaard insists, "There is an ignorance about one's own life that is tragic for the learned and for the simple, for both are bound by the same responsibility. This ignorance is called self-deceit."[22] Moreover, echoing Paine's point about the punitive nature of compliance strategies, Kierkegaard claims that a person motivated by fear turns all of life into an illness, insofar as fear of punishment cannot lead the person toward the Good but only serves as a sort of medicine administered in the wake of bad deeds.

After arguing forcefully against "barriers to willing one thing" such as egoism and weak commitment, Kierkegaard asserts that through contemplation and reflection one forms convictions which are stable even though there may be change on the surface. But how can one know that one's choice is not foolish pride, which ought to be accompanied by confession rather than confidence? (After all, many examples come to mind of hubris and of personal refusals to admit one's mistakes, sometimes with devastating results for others. Merton's journals, like *Conjectures*, are powerful and appealing, in part, because he openly discusses and struggles with self-doubt).[23] The most important thing of all, says Kierkegaard, is to "support righteousness and justice with self-sacrifice in the service of truth."[24] This too is Merton's conception of purity of heart. It encompasses not only unity of purpose but also a unity of perspective. The contemplative approach taken by Merton provides the foundation from which a deeper, holistic, "point of view of the universe" can be insightful. These three factors: unity of purpose, based on a depth of self-knowledge, and grasp of "the big picture," provided Merton—and can provide others—with a foundation for convictions that, while accepting of openness and recognizing the necessity of change, are nevertheless indicative of authentic leadership.

Merton, Moral Imagination, and Leadership

There are numerous other examples of leadership and moral imagination from Merton's life, in addition to the ones already discussed. At various points in his life Merton demonstrated features of leadership, both transformative, quiet, and otherwise. Arising from his contemplative practice, his leadership exhibited elements of self-knowledge, a vision of moral alternatives, and recognition of a deep unity with others. I will mention just a few examples, before turning to the natural link between the concept of moral imagination discussed in the previous chapter, qualities of authentic leadership, and their implications for professional ethics.

From the mid-1950s onward, Merton desired greater solitude. For years he had desired to live as a hermit at the monastery. In the wake of the enormous popularity of *Seven Storey Mountain*, the frequency of guests and visitors to Gethsemani, Merton had doubts as to whether or not he was best suited for life as a Trappist monk in the Cistercian Order. It was not that he found the daily routines too difficult or tedious, but in this Order, daily activities are done as a community. Consequently, he even considered leaving the order for one like the Carthusians, whose tradition permitted more privacy to monks. However, rather than undergoing the process of changing Orders and relocating, or receiving special treatment from the Order's leadership in Rome, or asking for a special favor from the abbot at Gethsemani, Merton decided to research the idea. He discovered that the Cistercian tradition actually had a history of allowing monks to live as hermits, though the practice had not been permitted in a very long time. In 1965, after persevering in his efforts, Merton was granted permission by the Order's leadership in Rome to live as a hermit. He subsequently moved to a one-room cement building in a wooded area near the monastery. Merton had successfully researched the issue and developed the justification for his request from the Order's own history. He even spread his interest in a life of solitude to others in the Order. Upon his retirement after Merton's death, the abbot of Gethsemani, James Fox, also took up the life of a hermit.

Another episode from Merton's life is reminiscent of Badaracco's concept of quiet leadership and wisdom: In 1962, Merton was silenced by his superiors for speaking out against war. Officials in the hierarchy of the church did not believe that war and other social-political issues were appropriate topics for a monk to be writing about; in their view it was contrary to a contemplative vocation of a monk. Merton naturally thought their perspective represented an ultimate form of guilty bystanding. Nevertheless, Merton submitted to the institutional leadership. Their instruction was that he not *publish* on the topic of war. Of course, this did not keep him from *writing* on the topic of war, which he continued to do in correspondences, in his journals, and in other essays. The caveat was that, since a "publisher" did not print these materials, then, technically, he was not "publishing" on the issue—actually, he was mimeographing and freely distributing them! In fact, these writings became published only later, some under the title, *Peace in the Post-Christian Era*, others more recently with the title, *The Cold War Letters*.[25] At the time, however, these writings received great circulation and much attention, perhaps in part due to their reputation as smuggled goods. The censorship, no doubt painful for Merton, could have been disheartening and could have squelched his creative and socially conscious voice. Instead, Merton exhibited some quiet leadership of his own by complying with the letter of the rule but creatively making enough room for freedom to maintain his integrity.

Another example illustrates the deep unity with others that Merton sensed, and even provides a glimpse into his own spiritual growth. In a passage from *Conjectures of a Guilty Bystander* with overtones of his epiphany, Merton walks through the monastery on night watch. But in contrast to the "fire watch" narrative recorded in *Sign of Jonas*, Merton thinks not of his own spiritual journey but that of the novices whom he mentors. Flashing the light across the dark, empty room, looking at the rows of desks in the silence of the darkness, Merton is filled with compassion for them and he contemplates the link between one's being and the place in which one works.[26] The better monks, Merton reasons, are those who strive to be most fully human, not those who struggle mightily to be grimly detached from others and suppress their humanity. Though the room is silent, dark and empty Merton senses the presence of the novices, being there in a spiritual way even though they were actually upstairs asleep. This space, though silent and dark, was the space in which they engaged their spiritual journeys, the space in which they work. Seeing the big picture gives one a sense of place and an awareness of the point of one's presence, of knowing "where" one is and having hope fused with prophetic vision as to how things will work out.

The notion that one's being, one's spiritual presence, can be felt in the space in which one works has interesting implications for professional ethics. Merton senses their presence as their novice master, he has a profound grasp of the strengths and weaknesses of each one, and appreciation for the dedication and limitations of each one, but as he puts it, "without flattery, without sentimentality, and without getting too involved in one another's business."[27] In his role as Master of Novices, Merton was not unlike a manager. Like a manager or human resources official, Merton guided these neophytes, wrote reports on their progress, and had a say in who was best qualified for promotion to the next level, who was best dismissed. Similar to responsibilities of a manager or CEO, the future of the organization, the quality of personnel guiding the organization forward, depended on his decisions. On his "night watch," Merton sensed their presence in the novitiate. Should a manager take the same view of the workplace? Several years ago, a management strategy dubbed "Management By Walking Around" (MBWA) sprang up; it is still quite popular.[28] MBWA is a means of developing better lines of communication between leadership personnel and others, getting management out of the confines in which groupthink occurs, to be in-touch with employees and other stakeholders. At worst, of course, it could be done in bad faith, a charade parallel to Sartre's waiter. At best, however, it provides a way of humanizing the workplace. The popular Dilbert cartoon often pokes fun of the common office cubicle and of the workspace created by a collection of them. Scott Adams, creator of the Dilbert character, has even designed the "ultimate cubicle," which he describes as fulfilling work's basic needs, "eat, sleep, and avoid the boss."[29] For anyone familiar with the Dilbert character, it is difficult to imagine his boss having the sort of experience had by Merton. It is a humanizing experience, a personalizing experience that acknowledges the spiritual presence of others and a profound awareness of a bigger picture, a deeper unity with others.

We have noted the ability of moral imagination to recognize linguistic schemas and metaphors which structure life, and much can be said about its relation to leadership. In his work *Hopeful Realism*, Douglas Ottati notes the connection between leadership and language.[30] He offers a devastating critique of "leadership speak," the jargon-laden, analogy-riddled doubletalk of so many leadership programs and consultants. Ottati unpacks a dominant metaphor of business leadership: sports. Competition is the key feature of the leadership and sports connection. Because business in a free-market economy can be so highly competitive, a setting in which excessive greed and desire for higher profitability sees the world in terms of winners and losers, leaders in business often turn to sports heroes for inspiration. Like the "package concept of love," however, this metaphor and the multiple analogies generated by it are not without negative impact and consequences. In this conceptual schema the prominent sensibility of a manager can be construed as manipulative in ways that exhibit bad faith. Indeed, the whole function of leadership from this point of view is to gain competitive advantage. This perspective may be applicable in a capitalistic society, but moral imagination can enable one to see alternative conceptions of our relationships to one another. What if we viewed each other as fellow travelers through life on this planet, in this space and during this time, not so much as competitors but fellow participants in life and death? What is the golden mean between competitiveness and solidarity? Moreover, the metaphors of business shape our lives in other ways, too, including politics. It is not simply the astronomical costs of campaigning for even lower level political offices that relegates seeking office to wealthy individuals; we have come to expect politicians to be good leaders if and because they have successful business experience.

Merton might be very critical of many contemporary leadership studies for being riddled with elements of bad faith. Recognizing this metaphor and of the negative implications of the other ones like it, it could be argued that genuine leadership involves selecting the conceptual schemas which structure experience for others. Hence, good leadership in business could mean the employment of metaphors and language which contribute to a positive and morally good workplace. Leadership involves the use of moral imagination to create an environment in which open discussions about ethical conflicts can take place, especially without the fear (much less reality) of retribution or disdain. With the aid of moral imagination, one can see that to not do this is to practice the logic of failure, allowing competitiveness to override moral sensitivities.

Merton further demonstrates leadership borne of moral imagination by developing some interesting concepts of his own. In the first chapter, I alluded to Merton's notion of an "overstimulated society." It is fascinating to ponder the implications of it for a wide variety of professions, especially the teaching profession. I recently had a conversation with a friend in the clergy; we were talking about technology and life in the twenty-first century. He said to me, "this must be a terrible time in history to be a philosopher." He explained his view by pointing out that people (particularly students) have television, radio, satellite radio, Internet, iPods, Blackberries, cell phones, and the list could go on. Information comes at us from so many different sources, constantly and simultaneously. Of course, my friend probably did not realize how close to accurate some people believe his statement to be. Some contemporary philosophers have astonishingly argued that "big P" Philosophy is exhausted as a discipline: there are no new discoveries to be made, grand theories to be developed or remarkable ideas remaining to be uncovered. Even one of my professors in graduate school would always introduce himself as a "historian of philosophy," not as a philosopher. But then the response came to me, so I replied to my friend, "There has never been a better time to be a philosopher." Looking at me in astonishment, I explained to him that philosophy is about critical reflection and at perhaps no other time in history have human beings been less reflective. As we strolled through the campus café, people were watching a news channel on television. The broadcaster was describing some live event while pictures and video continually popped up in boxes at the top of the screen. At the same time, across the bottom of the screen several lines of information streamed past. One line was relating financial information from stock markets across the world. The bottom line across the screen was relating other news stories (some of which seemed more interesting than the live event they were currently reporting). People in the café were watching all of this, many of them working at their laptops while talking on their Bluetooths about the music they just downloaded to their MP3 players. Not to be overlooked is that the television has well over one hundred channels available, many of those channels created to fill some market niche or due to complaints from customers eager for entertainment because at that moment "there isn't anything good on TV." Of course, the only thing worse than five channels with "nothing on" is to have one hundred fifteen more channels just like them. The myriad of options has even spawned new words, like "infotainment" for a show that is slightly informative and barely entertaining.

There are other examples; media is just one of the many ways in which Merton would say society is overstimulated. There is perhaps no better illustration of how we are overstimulated than as consumers. The diversity of products available to the ordinary person is remarkable, and there are typically multiple brands at hand for any given product. The variety of selections is staggering, almost overwhelming the consumer with the number of choices to be made for a simple single product. Take a careful look at your local pharmacy, choosing a cold remedy can be a grueling exercise in preference selection. For a given brand of over-the-counter medicine, one has numerous selections to make: sinus, cold, flu, congestion, runny nose, or cough formula? Regular dose or "maximum strength"? Tablets, liquid, gels or gel-caps? Cherry, orange or grape flavor? Sugar-free or not? Daytime or nighttime formula? I wanted the daytime, maximum strength, grape-flavored, liquid cough formula—but, of course, they are out of that one. So, now what should I do? Which preference should I compromise? How can I be truly satisfied if not all of my preferences are met? We become conditioned by this overstimulated environment. It shapes our expectations and fuels many of our frustrations. It sets the baseline for happiness. This is merely one of the many, many options that we face, as consumers, on a daily basis. Merton talks about "publicly approved" happiness that causes us to be discontented, unable to be satisfied with things easily in reach.[31]

This is Merton's concept of an overstimulated society. If he believed that we were overstimulated in the early 1960s—welcome to the twenty-first century! From shopping to sex, we clearly inhabit an overstimulated society. Sexual innuendo has become so commonplace in our culture, we hardly consciously (or conscientiously) notice anymore (an unquestionable appeal to passions and desires). So, there has perhaps never been a better time to be a philosopher, because it is increasingly difficult for people to find the space or time to engage in contemplation and critical self-reflection. When I was growing up, my father had a saying, "It is so noisy in this house I can't hear myself think!" Today's world is so noisy; the noise comes at us from all directions and from a variety of mediums, and much of the noise is self-inflicted. But it is so noisy one cannot hear one's self think. Merton calls us to a quiet moment in life, to solitude, to meditation which can stifle the noise of the world. It is not necessarily a call to world-denying solitude, it is more a call to a kind of *sabbath*, a time of rest and opportunity to drown out the noise of the world so that one can be refreshed to more actively and reflectively confront that world.

Seeing things from this lofty point of view may also clarify what Merton refers to in the *Conjectures of a Guilty Bystander* as "the myth of work." Merton contends that our society of business, "based on a pseudo-ethic of industriousness and thrift, to be rewarded by comfort, pleasure, and a good bank account," only leads to "an existence that is essentially meaningless and futile."[32] We have already noted the dominance of a "marketplace" metaphor in our capitalistic society, coming from its very foundation in the works of Adam Smith. Business, at least a great portion of it, according to Merton, is just so much "busy-ness" that we invent for ourselves, until we are "overwhelmed with jobs, duties, tasks, and assignments."[33] Reminiscent of a passage from Karl Marx's *Communist Manifesto* in which he mocks the way in which capital chases profit all over the world, Merton remarks on how we chase one another all around the world selling *ourselves*, attempting to escape the nothingness of our lives and to have our worth affirmed by the value which others place on us. The alienation and dehumanizing aspects of work can be analyzed by Marx and mocked by provocative media like Dilbert, but it takes the wisdom of contemplation exemplified by Merton's night watch experience to expose the myth of work and re-envision our spiritual presence in it.

This "busy-ness" of which Merton warns, highlights another feature of character that is important to moral imagination and leadership: the ability to change and grow, to mature in one's profession. Former President of Trinity College, Oxford and author Anthony Quinton points out that character is different from personality. The latter derives from the Latin word *persona*, which literally means a mask, something which like clothing can be put on, taken off or altered to suit one's preferences. Character goes much deeper, and though it can be modified (for example, through education and training), it is not as transparent or subject to change. "It is in essence resolution, determination," Quinton maintains, "a matter of pursuing purposes without being distracted by passing impulses." [34] This is evidenced not only by Merton's commitment to contemplative life and to religious devotion, but his commitment to what James Farrell calls Merton's personalism. Stemming from some of the radical movements of the 1960s in which activists confronted social institutions, including the Catholic worker movement, Merton's personalism highlights the importance of each individual in the eyes of God. Farrell recounts,

> Merton's personalism permeated his writing. 'The basic thing in Christian ethics,' he told Dorothy Day, 'is to look at the person and not at the nature. . . . Because when we consider nature we consider the general, the theoretical, and forget the concrete, the individual, the personal reality of the one confronting us. Hence we see him not as our other self, not as Christ, but as our demon, our evil beast, our nightmare."[35]

At the time of his death, Merton's understanding of his own vocation was that of a spiritual journey engaged in social action. It must be noted that neither his personalism nor his epiphany were starting-points or singular, isolated events. Merton's epiphany on a downtown street was not a "Damascus road" experience.[36] Rather, over time and through contemplative effort, Merton arrived at these perspectives and would have undoubtedly progressed beyond them were it not for his untimely death. Therefore, since his commitment and viewpoint grew and changed over time, we see in them something much deeper than personality, we see unity of purpose and perspective, hallmarks of wisdom and authentic leadership.

Transformation of Professional Life

For decades, even centuries, work has been the central feature of existence, the foremost activity around which people organize their lives. In part, this is surely because of the necessity of work to daily life. Though conceptualized in different ways, in the United States it was characterized as the Protestant work ethic. Thus, work has been linked inherently to one's self concept; who you are is a function of what you do. This was a natural attitude to have toward work. It was the way in which we spent much of our time, established acquaintances, gauged our personal success and measured our self-worth. For my father's generation, this was an explicit connection. This was borne out not only by their dedication and by a reverence for work, but also by their unspoken attitudes and simple customs. My father, and especially the men of his generation, would typically introduce themselves by including their line of work, almost immediately following mention of their names. Al Gini talks about this connection between work and self-identity in his book, *My Job, My Self*, in which he argues that individuality and self-identity were concepts associated with ordinary work for millions of people throughout the twentieth century.

However, it seems to me that there has been a movement away from this attitude, this ethic, in recent years. It is not that people do not work as hard, research and statistics show that people are working as hard as ever. It is not even that people are necessarily unhappy in their jobs, some research and commentators claim that alienation in the workplace is at an all-time low. However, I am beginning to doubt the current relevance of work as a measure of self-identity. If there is a shift away from this ethic, it may be due to a loss of employer loyalty to workers which has backfired and come full circle over time, so that now there is little employee loyalty to the workplace. Workers may feel less of a connection to or dedication for their employers, assuming (based on past experience both individually and collectively) that employers will show very little dedication to employees. Consumer electronics retailer, Circuit City may be a good example.[37] The result is that people opt for simplicity, not personally taking work seriously nor expecting work to take them seriously as persons. This may be particularly true of young people, those just entering the workforce as they graduate. They have already been told that it is likely for them to change *jobs*, not just places of employment, several times throughout their careers. The Japanese "Hodo-Hodo" are an example of this new attitude or ethic, a term which characterizes them as "slackers."[38] I suspect that the United States and Europe would have a comparable group of persons in the workforce, who approach things (particularly work) lackadaisically. Given that language communicates values, perhaps a different label would be given to this attitude in Western cultures, one that would not be as derogatory, based on an ethical relativism that attempts to treat all perspectives as equally valid. Work now becomes merely one aspect of life, which a person might approach with enthusiasm, indifference, or loathsomely, but without attaching any necessary meaning or significance to it. This allows one to simply go through the motions, like Sartre's waiter, unconcerned about either transcendence or bad faith. Work, for better or for worse, becomes relegated to one compartment of a heavily compartmentalized life. It becomes simply another facet of fragmentation of the self, which is so heavily criticized by MacIntyre, communitarians, and some social critics.

Professional life is different, or one might argue at least that it should be different, from this new attitude and work ethic. The nature of work in a profession differs somewhat from other types of jobs. Moreover, the level of commitment to a profession, especially commitment to others (let alone the additional education and training) makes it significantly different from the casual holding of a job, since the latter is characterized by no investment of the self and no trust of the employer beyond the next paycheck. As the Harvard researchers in the "Good Work" project discovered, when young professionals become disillusioned, the tendency is to change career choices. The testimony of professional accountant—turned Jesuit priest—James Martin is evidence of this trend. He was largely influenced by the spiritual journey of Merton. If their circumstances permit, even non-professionals in ordinary jobs choose to opt out and change jobs (professions, if necessary) when they become alienated and dissatisfied, in order to preserve a sense of meaning, purpose, and self-integrity. Martin is simply one example, among many.

In his book, *Becoming Who You Are*, James Martin provides a compelling narrative of his personal journey from high-paid, New York corporate accountant to Jesuit priest.[39] Although he does not use the terms of "bad faith" and "authenticity" as I have, he does speak passionately about the search for his "true self" and the inspiration that he received from reading Merton's works. Martin refers to his narrative as "the story of a corporate soul." He recounts his minimally religious childhood and early adulthood entry into the accounting profession, after graduating from the prestigious Wharton School of Business at the University of Pennsylvania. Although his life had every indication of success and personal satisfaction at the time, Martin felt increasingly dissatisfied and alienated from his profession. He became disillusioned by the circular logic of working so that he could make money, making money so that he could go to work. "I was miserable," Martin states, "overworked, stressed, lonely, and feeling trapped."[40] While "channel surfing" one evening, he happened across a PBS documentary about Thomas Merton. He found in the story of Merton, and later his writings, a fellow sojourner in search of a true self. As he puts it, "Merton had given my feelings a language."[41] The contemplative insights of Merton drew James Martin toward a distinction between one's true self, characterized by a struggle for authenticity and integrity, and one's false self, mired in bad faith and passive indifference.

The spiritual journey of James Martin is indicative of the connection that I am attempting to make between Merton's call to contemplation and the professional life. In trying to describe the difference between true selves and false ones, rather than relying on the philosophical language of authenticity and bad faith, Martin characterizes the difference between them in this way, "simply put, one attempts to move away from those parts of ourselves that prevent us from being closer to God."[42] This is very consistent with the Christian existentialism of Søren Kierkegaard but dramatically different from the atheistic view of Sartre.

For the sake of argument, let's call the theistic view of Kierkegaard, who sees the meaning of life an inherently intertwined with the existence of God, as the "strong position," since it has a strong theistic component. Let's call the search for authenticity and meaning in the absence of belief in God, the "weak position," since religious commitment holds a weak (or non-existent) position in this view. There is no question that Merton would side with the strong view of Kierkegaard and oppose the shortcomings of Sartre's weak perspective. However, when one compares the early writings of Merton, for example his best-selling autobiographical, *Seven Storey Mountain*, to his later writings, then it is clear that the mature Merton is more tolerant of views that differ from his own. This is, I believe, a testament to the power of his contemplative life and the wisdom of his spiritual journey. As mentioned before, Merton's spiritual experience was not a "Damascus road" occurrence, and this is relevant considering, "it is hard to do a great thing suddenly." This recognition is even more important, I believe, because of Merton's desire to meet people "where they are" in their personal quests for meaning, finding within himself a capacity for grasping a fundamental unity with all persons, those who might side with Kierkegaard or those who have more in common with Sartre. Thus, I do not think it is necessary for a person to share James Martin's metaphysical commitments, the strong position that is obviously similar to Kierkegaard's and to Merton's, nor to choose beforehand between the strong view or the weak position. In other words, I do not believe that one must have a metaphysical commitment to the belief in God in order to value the contribution of both James Martin's and Thomas Merton's conceptions of authenticity. So, whether I am "searching for my true self in God" or striving to actualize by higher degree of authenticity and purposefulness in my life, for the sake of argument I will take the weak position. Even from the weak position, I believe that Merton's point of view and its application to professional life can have profound consequences for our search for meaning and purpose in life, especially in the work that we do. For those who hold the stronger position, the connection between spiritual and professional life may be an even greater one; many spiritual persons have a sense of "calling" to a profession, a belief that there is a natural fit between the needs of society of their special gifts, which is not accidental nor by chance.

Regardless of whether one takes the strong view or the weaker version, it is clear that many people are torn between the demands of professional life and the search for wholeness in their personal lives. As the research from the Harvard study makes clear, some people find themselves caught between an unfulfilling career in a profession that they studied and trained in, perhaps even felt a special "calling" to, only to discover that their chosen walk of life has led them to a dead end, a deserted place with no address or sense of belonging. Nevertheless, for some of these people, a vestige of that call, perhaps with the metaphysical commitments of the stronger version in tow, still remains and thus they do not want to change careers. Hence, they live out the daily routine of their professional commitments in bad faith, passive indifference, or both. What the journey of Thomas Merton shows us, not only his words but also his deeds and character, is the importance of perseverance on that journey and the value of contemplation to the quest for authenticity and finding one's true self.

Merton's experience also demonstrates that, aside from fictional Hollywood stories which portray "city slickers" finding instant enlightenment and personal fulfillment through a quick vacation to an intimidating environment, *finding that "one true thing" which brings meaning and purpose to life is not so easy*. Merton's journey was gradual, uneven, but progressive and deepening. Though one might wish for a "Damascus road" experience, Merton's life and writings illustrate ways in which commitment and perseverance trump the instant and ostentatious. Even if a person managed to isolate a single belief or principle identified as that one true thing, it would still seem difficult to completely maintain one's existence with this sole focus. The result might be a rather narrow life, artificially constricted and closed to broader experiences and interests. Such a life might be possible and rewarding for some persons, but for many people who attempt to juggle the responsibilities of families, careers, civic and social interests, revolving all of one's life around a singularity may seem a bit far-fetched. We have discussed the problematic nature of the self and search for wholeness. Even Merton wrestled with competing interests and values throughout his spiritual journey, enjoying the recognition and attention of people around the world yet desiring more solitude and a hermit's life. So finding that one true thing may be difficult, but living life wholly in the light of it seems even more problematic. Merton's example of leadership demonstrates one way in which contemplative reflection can lead toward an authentic and integrated sense of self.

The desire to find one's true self, to live in the light of "one true thing," should therefore not mean jettisoning one's self-identity to a profession. As Sartre argues and his examples illustrate, our being always transcends the roles that we happen to occupy. So, one should not be a mere "cog in a machine" nor an automaton of a bureaucratic organization, expected to check one's self-identity and conscience at the door. Hence, Merton's example of a *journey* toward the true self can serve as a model not only for someone focusing narrowly on spirituality but also for someone who is grappling for a deeper understanding of the struggle to integrate professional values and commitments into one's life in a way that is complementary to the whole of one's existence, one's spiritual life. Moreover and perhaps most importantly, Merton's life and words are inspirational for anyone groping on this journey because he reinforces the reality that you are not alone. Other persons, just like you, struggle every day with the tensions and conflicts between professional responsibilities and personal moral values. I like it that Merton never left the Cistercian order; to be sure, he desired greater solitude at various times after coming to Gethsemani, he even explored the possibility of joining a different order—but, he never did. What I like about this is: The Cistercians at Gethsemani do everything as a community, and even when Merton needed the solitude of a hermit, he still participated in some communal activities of the monastery. The significance of community for finding a unity of the self with others is obvious.

However, community is important for other reasons, too. There are times when a person cannot speak out, cannot stand up for what is right over what is expedient, cannot challenge the soul battering organizational hierarchies that structure professional life. Sometimes they cannot speak because of difficult circumstances, or may not be able to stand up for being weighed down by personal pressures. Members of professions form a certain kind of community, and like-minded professionals should support one another during those times when speaking out and standing up are too painful or too risky to be done alone. An analogy from Sunday worship services may clarify this point. On any given Sunday morning, the cathedral has a throng of worshippers singing hymns and offering praise. But if we could know the innermost thoughts and secret concerns of many people scattered throughout that crowd, we would probably discover that their worries ensure that they do not feel like singing, they do not feel like praising. So, the others who are there, in a vicarious way, sing the hymns and offer the praises for those whose suffering and whose concerns would keep them away but for the restoration and rejuvenation which they find as part of the community. The hymns and praises of the community serve to lift the spirits of those who are suffering and down-hearted.

Professionals need to be this supportive of one another. Professionals of every sort need to exhibit a spirit of solidarity, especially through difficult situations in which an individual's moral values and commitments are stretched to their limits. This, too, is a part of the insight which one gleans from Merton and which can be nurtured through contemplation and self-reflection. Doing so carries the hope of transforming the relationship between work and self-identity and renewing the promises of professional life.

NOTES

Chapter One

[1] Most notably by Lawrence S. Cunningham, the John A. O'Brien Professor of Theology at the University of Notre Dame and editor of *Thomas Merton, Spiritual Master* (New York: Paulist Press, 1992).
[2] The Genovese case introduced the concept of the "bystander effect" (also known as "bystander apathy" or the "Genovese syndrome") to the field of Psychology. Although the reporting has been criticized, the case gained notoriety from the article, "38 Who Saw Murder Didn't Call Police," *New York Times*, March 27, 1964.
[3] Thomas Merton, *Conjectures of a Guilty Bystander* (New York: Doubleday, 1989), 156-158.
[4] Thomas Merton, *The Courage for Truth*, ed. Christine M. Bochen (New York: Farrar, Straus, Giroux, 1993), 62.
[5] Paul Pearson, "Innocent Bystander—Guilty Bystander: Thomas Merton's Monastic Option" (conference presentation, Merton and Moral Reflection in the Professions, Bellarmine University, Louisville, KY, March 10, 2006).
[6] Merton, *Conjectures*, 97.
[7] Merton, *Conjectures*, 231.
[8] *The Razor's Edge*, DVD, directed by John Byrum (Sony, 1984).
[9] Merton, *Conjectures*, 144.
[10] George O'Leary was the former long-time head football coach of the University of Georgia, who was briefly appointed to the more prestigious head coaching position at Notre Dame, until it was discovered that, in his application for his position at Georgia decades earlier, he engaged in "resume enhancement." A similar charge was brought against Marilee Jones, the widely praised guru of college admissions at MIT, whose career was cut short by revelations that she too had padded her resume, years earlier, when applying for an initial, low-level job with the university.
[11] *TIME*, "How To Speak Like a Real Republican," January 27, 2007.
[12] Ludwig Wittgenstein, *Tractatus Logico-Philosophicus*, trans. D. F. Pears and B. F. McGuinness (London: Routledge, 1955), 5.6.
[13] Merton, *Conjectures*, 16.
[14] Ibid.
[15] Merton, *Conjectures*, 20.
[16] Merton, *Conjectures*, 241.
[17] Merton, *Conjectures*, 248.
[18] Merton, *Conjectures*, 47.
[19] Ibid.

Chapter Two

[1] Merton, *Conjectures*, 153.
[2] Thomas Hobbes, *Leviathan* (Oxford: Oxford University Press, 1998).
[3] Peter Singer, *Rethinking Life and Death: The Collapse of Our Traditional Ethics* (New York: St. Martin's Press, 1994).
[4] Immanuel Kant, *The Metaphysics of Morals*, in *Practical Philosophy*, The Cambridge Edition of the Works of Immanuel Kant, trans. and ed. Mary J. Gregor (Cambridge: Cambridge University Press, 1996), 370.
[5] Kant, *Metaphysics of Morals*, 552.
[6] Merton, *Conjectures*, 98.
[7] Merton, *Conjectures*, 46.
[8] Merton, *Conjectures*, 118.
[9] Merton, *Conjectures*, 121.
[10] Allan Bloom, *The Closing of the American Mind* (New York: Simon & Schuster, 1987).
[11] Friedrich Nietzsche, *Untimely Meditations*, "The Uses and Disadvantages of History of Life" (Cambridge: Cambridge University Press, 1983), 62.
[12] Ibid.
[13] Alasdair MacIntyre, *After Virtue: A Study in Moral Theory* (Notre Dame: University of Notre Dame Press, 1984), 190.
[14] MacIntyre, *After Virtue*, 191.
[15] MacIntyre, *After Virtue*, 205-6.
[16] Aristotle, *Politics* 1253a27.
[17] Merton, *Conjectures*, 143.
[18] Merton, *Conjectures*, 33.
[19] Jose Ortega y Gassett, *Man and Crisis*, trans. Mildred Adams (New York: Norton, 1962), 200. Italics are mine.
[20] Charles Taylor, *Ethics of Authenticity* (Boston: Harvard University Press, 2007).
[21] Erich Auerbach, *Mimesis: The Representation of Reality in Western Literature*, trans. William R. Trask (Princeton: Princeton University Press, 1953), 549. This is especially clear at 535-7. Italics are mine.
[22] Alasdair MacIntyre, *Three Rival Versions of Moral Inquiry* (Notre Dame: University of Notre Dame Press, 1990), 149.
[23] Merton, *Conjectures*, 114.
[24] Merton, *Conjectures*, 144.
[25] See Matthew 10:39.
[26] Merton, *Conjectures*, 210.
[27] Peter Singer, *Practical Ethics* (Cambridge: Cambridge University Press), 314.
[28] Merton, *Conjectures*, 209.
[29] Anne E. Carr, *A Search for Wisdom and Spirit: Thomas Merton's Theology of the Self* (Notre Dame: University of Notre Dame Press, 1988), 73.
[30] Merton, *Conjectures*, 219.

Chapter Three

[1] Jean-Paul Sartre, *Being and Nothingness*, trans. Hazel E. Barnes (New York: Washington Square Press, 1966).
[2] MacIntyre, *After Virtue*, 191.
[3] Ibid.
[4] Sartre, *Being and Nothingness*, 97.
[5] Sartre, *Being and Nothingness*, 102.
[6] Merton, *Conjectures*, 49, 150, 265.
[7] William H. Simon, *The Practice of Justice: A Theory of Lawyers' Ethics* (Cambridge: Harvard University Press, 1998) 4 and 163.
[8] The example may be "extreme" in that few attorneys may ever face it, however, it has happened recently and not with good results. See Adam Liptak, "When Law Prevents Righting a Wrong," *New York Times*, May 4, 2008. The story is available online: http://www.nytimes.com/2008/05/04/weekinreview/04liptak.html?_r=2&pagewanted=1 (accessed November 28, 2008).
[9] Simon, *The Practice of Justice*, 4 and 164.
[10] Third episode, *The Decalogue*, DVD, directed by Krzysztof Kieslowski (Facets, 1988).
[11] Jeff Schmidt, *Disciplined Minds: A Critical Look at Salaried Professionals and the Soul-Battering System that Shapes Their Lives* (New York: Rowman and Littlefield, 2000), 2.
[12] Al Gini, *My Job, My Self: Work and the Creation of the Modern Individual* (New York: Routledge, 2000), 47.
[13] See *Damaged Care*, DVD, co-produced by Laura Dern (Paramount, 2001).
[14] Daniel Vallero and Jonathan T. Simpson, *Biomedical Ethics for Engineers: Ethics and Decision Making in Biomedical and Biosystems Engineering* (Amsterdam: Elsevier, 2007).
[15] Merton, *Conjectures*, 218.
[16] Merton, *Conjectures*, 184.
[17] Merton, *Conjectures*, 185.
[18] Ibid.
[19] Brian J. Mahan, *Forgetting Ourselves On Purpose: Vocation and the Ethics of Ambition* (San Francisco: Jossey-Bass, 2002), 90.
[20] Francis Fukuyama, *Trust: The Social Virtues and the Creation of Prosperity* (New York: Simon & Schuster, 1996).
[21] Eric Mount, Jr., *Professional Ethics in Context: Institutions, Images and Empathy* (Louisville: Westminster/John Knox Press, 1990), 44.
[22] Merton, *Conjectures*, 257.
[23] Schmidt, *Disciplined Minds*, 16-17.
[24] Dietrich Dorner, *The Logic of Failure: Recognizing and Avoiding Error in Complex Situations*, trans. Rita and Robert Kimber (New York: Metropolitan Books, 1996).
[25] See Thomas Friedman, "All Fall Down," *New York Times*, November 26, 2008.
[26] Merton, *Conjectures*, 165.

[27] Thomas Merton, *Raids on the Unspeakable* (New York: New Directions, 1966), 47.
[28] Martin Luther King, Jr., "Letter from a Birmingham Jail," (April 16, 1963). Available online at, http://www.thekingcenter.org/prog/non/Letter.pdf (accessed November 28, 2008).
For Merton's comments on King's "Letter," see *Conjectures*, 301.
[29] Merton, *Conjectures*, 58.
[30] Merton, *Conjectures*, 219.
[31] For example, Merton, *Conjectures*, 261.
[32] Merton, *Conjectures*, 264.
[33] Wendy Fischman, Becca Solomon, Deborah Greenspan and Howard Gardner, *Making Good: How Young People Cope With Moral Dilemmas at Work* (Cambridge: Harvard University Press, 2004).
[34] Schmidt, *Disciplined Minds*, 123.
[35] Fischman, et al., *Making Good*, 89.
[36] Merton, *Conjectures*, 118.
[37] Gini, *My Job, My Self*, 2.
[38] Mount, *Professional Ethics in Context*, 35.
[39] Schmidt, *Disciplined Minds*, 2.
[40] Fischman, et al., *Making Good*, 142.
[41] David Callahan, *The Cheating Culture: Why More Americans are Doing Wrong to Get Ahead* (New York: Harcourt, 2004), 84. Parenthetical comment is mine.
[42] Merton, *Conjectures*, 287-288.

Chapter Four

[1] Merton, *Conjectures*, 228.
[2] "RIPS" stands for "**R**ealm (context), **I**ndividual **P**rocess (judgment) and **S**ituation (ethical issue), and comes from the American Physical Therapy Association. See, for example, the regular column, "Ethics in Action," *PT Magazine*. "DISORDER" stands for:
Define the dilemma, **I**nformation gathering, **S**ort out stakeholders, **O**ptions and outcomes, **R**ules and rights, **D**ecision time, **E**valuate effects, **R**eview and reconsider. This model was developed by Lisa Newton, director of Program in Applied Ethics at Fairfield University, Fairfield, CT.
[3] See Robert M. Veatch, *The Basics of Bioethics*, 2nd ed. (Upper Saddle River: Prentice-Hall/Pearson, 2002); Veatch and Sara T. Fry, *Case Studies in Nursing Ethics*, 3rd ed. (London: Jones and Bartlett, 2006); Veatch and Harley E. Flack, *Case Studies in Allied Health Ethics* (Upper Saddle River: Prentice-Hall, 1997).
[4] Carl Elliot, *A Philosophical Disease: Bioethics, Culture and Identity*, Reflective Bioethics (New York: Routledge, 1999), 124.
[5] Elliot, *Philosophical Disease*, 125.
[6] Ibid.
[7] Ibid.
[8] Merton, *Conjectures*, 119.
[9] Lynn Sharp Paine, "Managing for Organizational Integrity" in *Harvard Business*

Review on Corporate Ethics (Cambridge: Harvard Business School Press, 2003), 87.
[10] Paine, "Organizational Integrity," 95.
[11] Lori Rackl, "Did SIU Profs Cheat On State Ethics Exam?" *Chicago Sun-Times*, January 4, 2007.
[12] Reuters, "SIUC Professor/IEA Win Battle Over State Ethics Test," April 29, 2008, http://www.reuters.com/article/pressRelease/idUS208019+29-Apr-2008+PRN20080429 (accessed November 30, 2008).
[13] Merton, *Conjectures*, 173.
[14] Patricia Werhane, *Moral Imagination and Management Decision Making* (Oxford: Oxford University Press, 1998), 36.
[15] Robert C. Solomon, *True to Our Feelings: What Our Emotions Are Really Telling Us* (Oxford: Oxford University Press, 2007), 204.
[16] Albert R. Jonsen and Stephen Toulmin, *The Abuse of Casuistry: A History of Moral Reasoning* (Berkeley: University of California Press, 1988), 5.
[17] Mark Johnson, *Moral Imagination: Implications of Cognitive Science for Ethics* (Chicago: University of Chicago Press, 1993), ix.
[18] Johnson, *Moral Imagination*, x.
[19] Johnson, *Moral Imagination*, 191.
[20] Marc D. Hauser, *Moral Minds: The Nature of Right and Wrong* (New York: Harper Perennial, 2007), 225.
[21] Hauser, *Moral Minds*, 235.
[22] Thomas Merton, *Love and Living*, ed. Naomi Burton Stone and Patrick Hart (New York: Farrar Straus Giroux, 1979; San Diego: Harcourt Brace Jovanovich, 1985), 29.
[23] Johnson, *Moral Imagination*, 157.
[24] Laura L. Nash, *Good Intentions Aside: A Manager's Guide to Resolving Ethical Problems* (Boston: Harvard Business School Press, 1993), 121.
[25] James R. Otteson, *Adam Smith's Marketplace of Life* (Cambridge: Cambridge University Press, 2002), 170 and 258.
[26] Johnson, *Moral Imagination*, 200.
[27] Johnson, *Moral Imagination*, 199.
[28] Johnson, *Moral Imagination*, 201.

Chapter Five

[1] Bernard M. Bass, *Transformational Leadership: Industry, Military, and Educational Impact* (Mahwah, NJ: Lawrence Erlbaum Associates, 1998).
[2] Bernard Bass and Paul Steidlmeier, "Ethics, Character, and Authentic Transformational Leadership," *Leadership Quarterly* 2 (1999): 181-217.
[3] Bass and Steidlmeier, "Ethics," 185.
[4] Joseph Badaracco, *Leading Quietly: An Unorthodox Guide to Doing the Right Thing* (Boston: Harvard Business School Press, 2002), 10.
[5] Badaracco, *Leading Quietly*, 51.
[6] *Pirates of the Caribbean: The Curse of the Black Pearl*, DVD, directed by Gore Verbinski (Walt Disney Video, 2005).

[7] Badaracco, *Leading Quietly*, 149.
[8] James Davidson Hunter, *The Death of Character: Moral Education in an Age Without Good or Evil* (New York: Basic Books, 2000).
[9] James Q. Wilson, *The Moral Sense* (New York: Simon & Schuster, 1993).
[10] John Kekes, "Wisdom" in *Oxford Companion to Philosophy*, ed. Ted Honderich (Oxford: Oxford University Press, 1995).
[11] John Kekes, *The Examined Life* (Cranbury, NJ: Associated University Presses, 1988), 152.
[12] See Christopher Peterson and Martin Seligman, *Character Strengths and Virtues: A Handbook and Classification* (Oxford: Oxford University Press, 2004). Martin Seligman has written extensively on the key concept, "positive psychology."
[13] Merton, *Conjectures*, 65, 120.
[14] Merton, *Conjectures*, 184.
[15] Merton, *Conjectures*, 156.
[16] Merton, *Conjectures*, 158.
[17] Ronald R. Sims, *Ethics and Organizational Decision Making: A Call for Renewal* (Westport: Quorum Books, 1994), 66.
[18] Lawrence S. Cunningham, *Thomas Merton and the Monastic Vision*, Library of Religious Biography (Grand Rapids: Eerdmans, 1999).
[19] Cunningham, *Monastic Vision*, 107.
[20] *City Slickers*, DVD, directed by Ron Underwood (MGM, 1991).
[21] See Matthew 5:8.
[22] Søren Kierkegaard, *Purity of Heart is to Will One Thing: Spiritual Preparation for the Office of Confession*, trans. Douglas Steere (New York: Harper & Row, 1956), 52.
[23] Merton, *Conjectures*, 49, 261-262, 271.
[24] Kierkegaard, *Purity of Heart*, 113.
[25] Thomas Merton, *Peace in the Post-Christian Era*, ed. Patricia A. Morton (Maryknoll: Orbis Books, 2004); Thomas Merton, *Cold War Letters*, ed. William H. Shannon (Maryknoll: Orbis Books, 2007).
[26] Merton, *Conjectures*, 213.
[27] Merton, *Conjectures*, 214.
[28] See for example, http://pmcrunch.com/project_management_process/mbwa-managing-by-walking-around-what-it-is-and-what-it-is-not/.
[29] http://archives.cnn.com/2001/CAREER/jobenvy/08/28/dilbert.scott.adams/index.html.
[30] Douglas Ottati, *Hopeful Realism: Reclaiming the Poetry of Theology* (Cleveland: The Pilgrim Press, 1999), 7-21.
[31] Merton, *Conjectures*, 56.
[32] Merton, *Conjectures*, 195.
[33] Ibid.
[34] Anthony Quinton, "Character and Culture," *New Republic* 189, no. 16 (1983): 26-30.
[35] James T. Farrell, "Thomas Merton and the Religion of the Bomb," *Religion and American Culture* 5, no. 1 (1995): 83.

[36] I have already discussed transitions in the titles and content of his writings, as evidence of this claim. However, passages from *Conjectures* alone support this view. One can find similar "epiphanies" in *Conjectures*, both "early" and "late." See *Conjectures*, 144, 156, 212.

[37] See, Doug Desjardins, "Circuit City Re-org Results in 3,400 Layoffs," *Retailing Today* 46 (April 9, 2007), 3. For a very critical analysis of their decision, see, John Hollon, "And the nominees are . . . ?" *Workforce Management* 86 (April 9, 2007), 34.

[38] Hiroko Tabuchi, "Slacker Nation? Young Japanese Shun Promotions," *Wall Street Journal*, November 1, 2008.

[39] James Martin, SJ, *Becoming Who You Are: Insights on the True Self from Thomas Merton and Other Saints*, (Boston: Hidden Spring, 2006).

[40] Martin, *Becoming Who You Are*, 14.

[41] Martin, *Becoming Who You Are*, 17.

[42] Martin, *Becoming Who You Are*, 22.

BIBLIOGRAPHY

Auerbach, Erich. *Mimesis: The Representation of Reality in Western Literature*. Translated by William R. Trask. Princeton: Princeton University Press, 1953.

Badaracco, Joseph. *Leading Quietly: An Unorthodox Guide to Doing the Right Thing*. Boston: Harvard Business School Press, 2002.

Bass, Bernard M. *Transformational Leadership: Industry, Military, and Educational Impact*. Mahwah, NJ: Lawrence Erlbaum Associates, 1998.

Bass, Bernard M., and Paul Steidlmeier. "Ethics, Character, and Authentic Transformational Leadership." *Leadership Quarterly* 2 (1999): 181-217.

Bloom, Allan. *The Closing of the American Mind*. New York: Simon & Schuster, 1987.

Callahan, David. *The Cheating Culture: Why More Americans are Doing Wrong to Get Ahead*. New York: Harcourt, 2004.

Carr, Anne E. *A Search for Wisdom and Spirit: Thomas Merton's Theology of the Self*. Notre Dame: University of Notre Dame Press, 1988.

City Slickers, DVD. Directed by Ron Underwood. MGM, 1991.

Cunningham, Lawrence S. *Thomas Merton, Spiritual Master*. New York: Paulist Press, 1992.

—. *Thomas Merton and the Monastic Vision*, Library of Religious Biography (Grand Rapids: Eerdmans, 1999).

Damaged Care, DVD. Co-produced by Laura Dern. Paramount, 2001.

Dörner, Dietrich. *The Logic of Failure: Recognizing and Avoiding Error in Complex Situations*. Translated by Rita and Robert Kimber. New York: Metropolitan Books, 1996.

Elliot, Carl. *A Philosophical Disease: Bioethics, Culture and Identity*, Reflective Bioethics. New York: Routledge, 1999.

Farrell, James T. "Thomas Merton and the Religion of the Bomb." In *Religion and American Culture* 5, no. 1 (1995): 77-98.

Fischman, Wendy, and Becca Solomon, Deborah Greenspan and Howard Gardner, *Making Good: How Young People Cope With Moral Dilemmas at Work*. Cambridge: Harvard University Press, 2004.

Friedman, Thomas. "All Fall Down," Editorial. *New York Times*, November 26, 2008.
Fukuyama, Francis. *Trust: The Social Virtues and the Creation of Prosperity*. New York: Simon & Schuster, 1996.
Gini, Al. *My Job, My Self: Work and the Creation of the Modern Individual*. New York: Routledge, 2000.
Hauser, Marc D. *Moral Minds: The Nature of Right and Wrong*. New York: Harper Perennial, 2007.
Hobbes, Thomas. *Leviathan*. Oxford: Oxford University Press. 1998.
Hunter, James Davidson. *The Death of Character: Moral Education in an Age Without Good or Evil*. New York: Basic Books, 2000.
Johnson, Mark. *Moral Imagination: Implications of Cognitive Science for Ethics*. Chicago: University of Chicago Press, 1993.
Jonsen, Albert R. and Stephen Toulmin, *The Abuse of Casuistry: A History of Moral Reasoning*. Berkeley: University of California Press, 1988.
Kant, Immanuel. *Practical Philosophy*, The Cambridge Edition of the Works of Immanuel Kant. Translated and edited by Mary J. Gregor. Cambridge: Cambridge University Press, 1996.
Kekes, John. *The Examined Life*. Cranbury, NJ: Associated University Presses, 1988.
—. "Wisdom." In *Oxford Companion to Philosophy*. Edited by Ted Honderich. Oxford: Oxford University Press, 1995.
Kierkegaard, Søren. *Purity of Heart is to Will One Thing: Spiritual Preparation for the Office of Confession*. Translated by Douglas Steere. New York: Harper & Row, 1956.
King, Jr., Martin Luther. "Letter from a Birmingham Jail," (April 16, 1963). Available online at, http://www.thekingcenter.org/prog/non/Letter.pdf. Accessed November 28, 2008.
Liptak, Adam. "When Law Prevents Righting a Wrong," *New York Times*, May 4, 2008.
MacIntyre, Alasdair. *After Virtue: A Study in Moral Theory*. Notre Dame: University of Notre Dame Press, 1984.
—. *Three Rival Versions of Moral Inquiry*. Notre Dame: University of Notre Dame Press, 1990.
Mahan, Brian J. *Forgetting Ourselves On Purpose: Vocation and the Ethics of Ambition*. San Francisco: Jossey-Bass, 2002.
Martin, James, SJ. *Becoming Who You Are: Insights on the True Self from Thomas Merton and Other Saints*. Boston: Hidden Spring, 2006.
Merton, Thomas. *Conjectures of a Guilty Bystander*. New York: Doubleday, 1989.

—. *Cold War Letters*. Edited by William H. Shannon. Maryknoll: Orbis Books, 2007.
—. *Peace in the Post-Christian Era*. Edited by Patricia A. Morton. Maryknoll: Orbis Books, 2004.
—. *The Courage for Truth*. Edited by Christine M. Bochen. New York: Farrar, Straus, Giroux, 1993.
—. *Love and Living*. Edited by Naomi Burton Stone and Patrick Hart. San Diego: Harcourt Brace Jovanovich, 1985. First published in 1979 by Farrar Straus Giroux.
Mount, Jr., Eric. *Professional Ethics in Context: Institutions, Images and Empathy*. Louisville: Westminster John Knox Press, 1990.
Nash, Laura L. *Good Intentions Aside: A Manager's Guide to Resolving Ethical Problems*. Boston: Harvard Business School Press, 1993.
Nietzsche, Friedrich. *Untimely Meditations*. Cambridge: Cambridge University Press, 1983.
Ortega y Gassett, Jose. *Man and Crisis*. Translated by Mildred Adams. New York: Norton, 1962.
Ottati, Douglas. *Hopeful Realism: Reclaiming the Poetry of Theology*. Cleveland: The Pilgrim Press, 1999.
Otteson, James R. *Adam Smith's Marketplace of Life*. Cambridge: Cambridge University Press, 2002.
Paine, Lynn Sharp. "Managing for Organizational Integrity." In *Harvard Business Review on Corporate Ethics*. Cambridge: Harvard Business School Press, 2003.
Pearson, Paul. "Innocent Bystander—Guilty Bystander: Thomas Merton's Monastic Option." Conference presentation, Merton and Moral Reflection in the Professions, Bellarmine University, Louisville, KY, March 10, 2006.
Peterson, Christopher, and Martin Seligman, *Character Strengths and Virtues: A Handbook and Classification*. Oxford: Oxford University Press, 2004.
Pirates of the Caribbean: The Curse of the Black Pearl. DVD, directed by Gore Verbinski, Walt Disney Video, 2005.
Quinton, Anthony. "Character and Culture." In *New Republic* 189, no. 16 (1983): 26-30.
Rackl, Lori. "Did SIU Profs Cheat On State Ethics Exam?" *Chicago Sun-Times*, January 4, 2007.
Sartre, Jean-Paul. *Being and Nothingness*. Translated by Hazel E. Barnes. New York: Washington Square Press, 1966.

Schmidt, Jeff. *Disciplined Minds: A Critical Look at Salaried Professionals and the Soul-Battering System that Shapes Their Lives.* New York: Rowman and Littlefield, 2000.
Simon, William H. *The Practice of Justice: A Theory of Lawyers' Ethics.* Cambridge: Harvard University Press, 1998.
Sims, Ronald R. *Ethics and Organizational Decision Making: A Call for Renewal.* Westport: Quorum Books, 1994.
Singer, Peter. *Practical Ethics.* Cambridge: Cambridge University Press.
—. *Rethinking Life and Death: The Collapse of Our Traditional Ethics.* New York: St. Martin's Press, 1994.
Smock, Frederick. *Pax Intrantibus: A Meditation on the Poetry of Thomas Merton.* Frankfort: Broadstone Books, 2007.
Solomon, Robert C. *True to Our Feelings: What Our Emotions Are Really Telling Us.* Oxford: Oxford University Press, 2007.
Taylor, Charles. *Ethics of Authenticity.* Boston: Harvard University Press, 2007.
The Decalogue. DVD. Directed by Krzysztof Kieslowski. Facets, 1988.
The Razor's Edge. DVD. Directed by John Byrum. Sony, 1984.
Vallero, Daniel, and Jonathan T. Simpson, *Biomedical Ethics for Engineers: Ethics and Decision Making in Biomedical and Biosystems Engineering.* Amsterdam: Elsevier, 2007.
Veatch, Robert M. *The Basics of Bioethics.* Second edition. Upper Saddle River: Prentice-Hall/Pearson, 2002.
Veatch, Robert M. and Sara T. Fry. *Case Studies in Nursing Ethics.* Third edition. London: Jones and Bartlett, 2006.
Veatch, Robert M. and Harley E. Flack. *Case Studies in Allied Health Ethics.* Upper Saddle River: Prentice-Hall, 1997.
Werhane, Patricia. *Moral Imagination and Management Decision Making.* Oxford, Oxford University Press, 1998.
Wilson, James Q. *The Moral Sense.* New York: Simon & Schuster, 1993.
Wittgenstein, Ludwig. *Tractatus Logico-Philosophicus.* Translated by D. F. Pears and B. F. McGuinness. London: Routledge, 1955.

INDEX

A
A Search for Wisdom and Spirit (Carr), 33
academic
   honesty, 50, 78
   profession, 3, 13, 40, 46, 48, 64, 84
After Virtue, (MacIntyre), 25
America, 4, 25, 28, 31, 72, 109
Apology (Plato), 107
Arendt, Hannah, 57
Aristotle, 14, 15, 20, 25, 27, 38, 75, 91, 96, 102, 106, 107
attorney-client privilege, 43
Auerbach, Erich, 30
authenticity, 32, 38, 40, 44, 47, 85, 101, 105, 118, 120, 122
autonomy, 2, 102

B
bad faith, 42, 47, 50, 53, 58, 74, 79, 81, 85, 100, 105, 107, 110, 113, 119
   description of, 39
   examples of, 40
   leadership mired in, 101
Badaracco, Joseph, 102
Bass, Bernard, 100
Becoming Who You Are (Martin), 120
Beech-Nut incident, 82
Bentham, Jeremy, 17, 86
bioethics, 46, 50, 79, 94
Bloom, Allan, 26, 52
burnout, 44, 96
business
   ethics, 9, 46, 73, 82, 108
   Merton's view of, 7, 20, 53

organizations, 47, 48, 51, 84, 93, 100, 108, 116
profession, 5, 9, 24, 46, 114
busy-ness, 117
bystanding, 5, 6, 38, 47, 54, 57, 81, 112

C
Callahan, David, 72
Carlin, George, 9, 87
Carr, Anne, 33
case studies
   in ethics training, 50, 55, 78, 80, 82
   scripted nature of, 79
   structure of, 77, 79, 95, 104
Challenger disaster, 55
Chambers, Tod, 79
chaotic forces, 41
character, 25, 52, 53, 71, 100, 105–7, 121
cheating, 50, 66, 81, 84
Chernobyl disaster, 55
Christian Socratism, 38, 56
Circuit City incident, 119
City Slickers, 110
civil disobedience, 59
codes of ethics, 2, 6, 24, 26, 34, 37, 44, 46, 51, 54, 58, 66, 73, 80, 83, 95, 101, 103
cognitive dissonance, 46, 71
communitarianism, 25, 27, 29, 31, 119
community
   concepts of, 8, 14, 32, 34, 68, 111, 123
   professions as, 5, 100, 123
competition, 63, 66, 68, 72, 114

compliance approach to ethics, 81–85, 105, 110
confidentiality, 43, 44
contemplation, 6, 15, 24, 37, 47, 53, 74, 95, 97, 98, 103, 106, 110, 116, 117, 120, 121, 122, 123
contempt for the world, 11, 21
context, 6, 8, 11, 20, 24, 39, 45, 47, 51, 53, 56, 63, 69, 79, 91, 95, 98, 101, 106
corporate ethics officers, 59
Crystal, Billy, 110
Cunningham, Lawrence, 109, 124

D
Damaged Care, v
daydream, 27, 31
deontology, 14, 17, 19, 22, 58, 69, 87, 97
dialectic, 15, 47, 48, 56, 74, 107
dilemmas, 42–46
  bioethical, 43, 95
  legal, 42
  scripting of, 79, 95, 98
  use in ethics training, 80, 89
Disciplined Minds (Schmidt), 44, 53, 69, 71
Dörner, Dietrich, 54
drunk driver incident, 87

E
egoism, 5, 14, 16, 21, 23, 27, 32, 55, 64, 72, 87, 97, 102, 110
Eichmann in Jerusalem (Arendt), 57
Eichmann, Adolf, 57, 84
Elliot, Carl, 79
emotions, 44, 63, 85–90, 92, 96
empathy, 92, 96
Enron incident, 55, 82
ethics
  and emotions, 85–90
  codes. *See* codes of ethics
  dilemmas, 3, 42–46, 62, 70, 92, 102, 109
  egoism, 5
  professional, 23–24
  theories of, 14–20, 37, 69, 107, 119
  training, 81, 84, 90
Ethics and Organizational Decision Making (Sims), 108
Ethics of Authenticity, (Taylor), 30
ethics of expediency, 82
Etzioni, Amitai, 29
euphemisms, 10
existentialism, 39, 40, 41, 120
Exxon *Valdez* incident, 55

F
Farrell, James, 117
Fischman, Wendy, 62, 96
forced systematization, 53, 54, 96
Ford Motor Co., 21
Forgetting Ourselves On Purpose (Mahan), 48
Fox, James, 112
fragmentation of the self, 24–27, 37, 42, 44, 47, 75, 119
freedom, 2, 11, 21, 27, 31, 39, 48, 52, 56, 58, 60, 65, 72, 85, 94, 101, 112
Fukuyama, Francis, 48

G
game
  ethics training as, 76, 78, 80, 84
  playing, in bad faith, 40, 45, 52
  theory, 54, 76
Gardner, Howard, 62
General Electric Co., 7
General Motors Co., 21
generations, 28, 29, 71, 118
genetics, 62, 63, 64, 66
Genovese syndrome, 5, 87
Genovese, Kitty, 55, 124
Gini, Al, 45, 70, 73, 118
golden mean, 15, 114
golden rule, 98
government regulation, 2, 43, 82
gray areas, 34, 59, 66
GRE exam, 53
greatest good, 17, 18, 33, 50, 86, 87

H
habits, 9, 15, 22, 45, 75–77, 81, 105
Hanks, Tom, 27
Harvard "Good Work" research, 62, 73
Hauser, Marc, 92, 97
healthcare profession, 33, 43, 79, 95, 104
hermit
   Merton's life as, 4, 7, 111, 122, 123
Hippocratic Oath, 45, 64, 94
Hobbes, Thomas, 16
holism (sense of self), 27–31, 34, 38, 41, 111
Hopeful Realism (Ottati), 114
human nature, 14, 16, 17, 38, 103, 105
Hume, David, 91, 97
Hunter, James Davidson, 105
Hurricane Katrina, 55
hybrid professionals, 45

I
ideology, 53, 60
inauthentic. *See* bad faith
informed consent, 94
institutional review boards, 59
integrity, 105
   approach to ethics, 81–85
   personal, 22, 48, 51, 53, 64, 68, 112, 119

J
Johnson & Johnson, 55
Johnson, Mark, 90, 92, 96
Jones, Marilee, 9, 124
Jonsen, Albert, 89
journalism profession, 67, 72

K
Kant, Immanuel, 17, 19, 22, 86, 97, 107
Kekes, John, 105
Kierkegaard, Søren, 110
Kieslowski, Krzysztof, 43, 47

King, Martin Luther, Jr., 19, 59
Kohlberg, Lawrence, 20

L
Laborem Exercens, 2
language, 8, 11, 19, 24, 30, 50, 69, 76, 79, 84, 91, 105, 114, 120
law (and legality), 19, 43, 58, 83, 88, 95
Leading Quietly (Badaracco), 102
legal profession, 33, 42, 82
Letter from a Birmingham Jail (King), 59
liberal arts education, 52
logic of failure, 5, 42, 56, 60, 79, 83, 85, 95, 106, 109, 114
   and bystanding, 58
   explanation of, 54
Logical Positivism, 10
love
   Merton's law of, 22
   of others, 33, 53, 105, 108
   package concept of, 93, 114
LSAT exam, 53

M
Maccoby, Michael, 70
MacIntyre, Alasdair, 26, 27, 29, 38, 39, 42, 47, 87, 91, 119
Mahan, Brian, 48
Making Good: How Young People Cope with Moral Dilemmas (Fischman), 62
management by walking around, 113
Marcel, Gabriel, 42
market
   as metaphor, 9, 58, 93, 117
   forces of, 62, 64, 65, 68, 70, 72, 114
market transaction
   love as, 93
Martin, James, 119
Marty, Martin, 109
Marx, Karl, 2, 117
McGraw, Phil ("Dr. Phil"), 50

Merton
- biography, 3–6
- epiphany, 5
- *Love and Living*, 93
- Master of Novices, 4, 73, 113
- *Peace in the Post-Christian Era*, 112
- *Raids on the Unspeakable*, 4, 57
- *Seven Storey Mountain*, 4, 111, 120
- *The Cold War Letters*, 112
- works by, 4

metaphors, 16, 21, 58, 90, 91, 92, 93, 95, 97, 106, 114, 117
Mimesis (Auerbach), 30
moral imagination
- description of, 90, 92
- in decision-making, 83, 85, 95, 103, 109
- in leadership, 84, 99, 114
- Merton and, 106, 111, 115

Moral Imagination (Johnson), 90
Moral Imagination and Management Decision Making (Werhane), 85
moral law, 59, 86, 87, 97
Moral Minds (Hauser), 92
motivation, 39, 66, 82, 89, 100
motives, 16, 19, 21, 33, 66, 88, 93, 96, 102
Mount, Eric, 52, 70, 92, 99
murder, 5, 43, 57
Murray, Bill, 7
My Job, My Self (Gini), 45, 70, 118
myth, 13, 27, 116

N
narrative sense of self, 26, 61, 90, 92, 112, 120
Nash, Laura, 93
Nicomachean Ethics (Aristotle), 91
Nietzsche, Friedrich, 22, 25, 98, 103
novices, 112

O
O'Leary, George, 9, 124

online ethics training, 81, 84
Oracle of Delphi, 107
Ortega y Gassett, Jose, 29
Ottati, Douglas, 114
Otteson, James, 97
overstimulated society, 20, 107, 115, 116

P
Paine, Lynn Sharp, 82
Palance, Jack, 110
passive indifference, 5, 47, 54, 56, 60, 101, 102, 105, 120, 121
Pax Intrantibus: A Meditation on the Poetry of Thomas Merton (Smock), vii
peace
- inner, 20, 32, 34
- opposed to war, 112

Pearson, Paul, 6
Peeno, Linda, 45
personal morality, 24, 26, 46, 71, 107, 122
personal morality and role morality, 24, 38–42
personalism, 117
personality, 52, 53, 56, 117, 118
Philosophical Disease (Elliot), 79
Pirates of the Caribbean, 103
Plato, 14, 20, 28, 52, 77, 90, 96, 107
playing the game, 40, 81
point of view of the universe, 32, 67, 108, 111
politics, 7, 10, 33, 60, 98, 112, 114
Pope John Paul II, 2
Pope John XXIII, 47
postmodernism, 8, 14, 25, 29, 31, 79, 105
profession
- academic, 40, 51
- as "well-aligned", 62
- as ideology, 53
- business, 9, 24
- definition of, 2
- genetics, 64
- healthcare, 33, 44, 104

hybrid, 45
journalism, 67
legal, 33, 34, 42
theater, 63
traits of, 23, 34, 42, 44, 77, 96, 119
progressivism, 105
protestant work ethic, 23, 118
public service, 2, 34
Purity of Heart (Kierkegaard), 110

Q

quiet leadership, 102–4
Quinton, Anthony, 117

R

radical freedom, 39, 41
Rand, Ayn, 17, 19
reasoned moral action, 82, 107
regulation, 2, 43, 46, 59, 60, 82
regulatory agencies, 59
relativism, 24, 25, 72, 119
Republic (Plato), 90
resume enhancement, 9, 124
Rethinking Life and Death (Singer), 18
Rodgers, Daniel, 24
role morality, 24, 26, 31, 37, 38–42, 49, 56, 75, 95
Ross, Sir David, 22

S

Sartre, Jean-Paul, 38, 42, 45, 47, 53, 74, 113, 119, 122
Schmidt, Jeff, 44, 47, 53, 65, 69, 99
Sears Auto Centers incident, 82
self
  actualization, 2, 24, 61, 69, 96, 120
  deception, 28, 110
  fragmentation of, 24, 37, 41, 42, 75, 119
  help, 9, 21, 34, 106
  identity, 20, 23, 27, 46, 51, 62, 69, 73, 91, 93, 118, 122

interest, 5, 16, 24, 32, 72, 97, 99, 101, 103
knowledge, 11, 21, 29, 38, 41, 47, 56, 59, 64, 81, 92, 96, 99, 105, 107, 116
  Merton's view of, 11, 21, 33, 41, 53, 99, 108, 111
  nature of, 121
  regulation, 60
  respect, 19
  unity of, 27, 28, 32, 42, 53, 91, 102, 123
shuttle *Challenger* disaster, 55
Simon, William, 42
Sims, Ronald, 108
Singer, Peter, 18, 32, 67, 108
Smith, Adam, 8, 93, 97, 117
Socratic, 15, 28, 38, 42, 47, 50, 56, 90, 94, 95, 106
Solomon, Robert, 86, 92, 98
submission to organized injustice, 56

T

Taylor, Charles, 29
telos, 25
The Abuse of Casuistry (Jonsen and Toulmin), 89
The Cheating Culture (Callahan), 72
The Closing of the American Mind (Bloom), 25
The Decalogue, 43
The Razor's Edge, 7
theater, 63
Theory of Moral Sentiments (Smith), 97
Thomas Merton and the Monastic Vision (Cunningham), 109
Three Rival Versions of Moral Inquiry (MacIntyre), 31
Toulmin, Stephen, 89
trust, 24, 49, 65, 70, 80, 86, 95, 102, 119
Trust (Fukuyama), 48
tyranny of principles, 89

U
universalizability, 19, 22, 97
Untimely Meditations (Nietzsche), 25
utilitarianism, 14, 17, 19, 22, 32, 57, 69, 87, 101, 106

V
Veatch, Robert, 79

W
virtue ethics, 14, 20, 25, 38, 75, 88
Wealth of Nations (Smith), 97
Werhane, Patricia, 85
whistle blowing, 50, 51
Wilson, James Q., 105
Wittgenstein, Ludwig, 10, 79
work
    as center of life, 23, 52, 53, 112, 118
    as meaningful, 2, 6, 60, 75, 99, 123
    as oppressive, 44, 96, 118
    Harvard study of, 60–74
    value of, 1

Z
Zimbardo experiment, 56